WORKING WAGONS

A pictorial review of freight stock
on the B.R. system.

by

David Larkin

Volume 4. 1985 to 1992

Santona Publications
Hull

Working Wagons

Volume 4. 1985 - 1992

First Published 2002

British Library Cataloguing-in-publication Data.
A catalogue record for this book is available from the British Library

First Published in 2002 by;
Santona Publications,
Rydal Mount,
224, Marlborough Avenue,
Hull. HU5 3LE.

Design & typesetting by Santona Publications.
Photographic printing by Steve Flint Photography, Hull.
Printed by The Amadeus Press Ltd.

ISBN 0 9538448 4 6.

WORKING WAGONS
Volume 4. 1985 - 1992

Contents

Contents

(continued)

Introduction

In terms of changes to the fleet, the final period covered in this series began with relatively little activity. From about 1988, the pace of change began to quicken and initial transformations occurred as a consequence of the recent relaunch of the freight business sub-Sectors. Further changes followed, such as those effected by the demise of Speedlink, until by 1992, the whole rail freight scene found itself on the verge of two historic upheavals which were to significantly affect wagon types; namely the opening of the Channel Tunnel and the Privatisation of British Rail.

In this fourth volume therefore, we take a look at wagons in the last period when the railway network still ascribed to being a public service industry. And where better to start than with the traditional fleet.

This had been virtually eliminated in terms of revenue-earning stock and only a few examples, as illustrated in Sections 1 to 3, survived in the departmental fleets. Even such rebuilds as the MTV opens (see Vol. 2 pg. 43) were now in C. E. stock (top right).

The still relatively new B.R. owned air braked fleet went through numerous transformations as a consequence of ever changing commercial markets. Many wagon types, only a few years old, had very short careers and soon found themselves being rebuilt to carry different commodities.

Relatively few totally new designs were built during the

Above. *DB390090 (Taken at Reading, 16/5/92)*
The MTV class had been used for stone and sand traffic and their bodywork was generally in good overall condition, making them a useful type for immediate use by the C.E. Livery is yellow/Rail Grey with black underframe and white lettering. Code is ZDV ZANDER, the name being painted in Rail Grey.
(Ref: W16912/DL)

review period. One that appeared, but not in production quantities, was a bogie steel coil carrier with nylon hood. This was built in three lengths, the BGAs (see below), which were numbered 961000 to 961003, the BHAs (962000 to 962003) and the BJAs (963000 to 963003).

In general, the bulk of the new types came from the rebuilding of existing ones, some of which were merely one-

Below. *961001 (Taken at RFS Doncaster, 26/6/92)*
The vehicle shown here carried steel coil and was similar to vehicles built for the private owners (see pages 78 and 84). Livery is Flame Red nylon hood with white lettering and squares, ends are black as are the frame and bogies, lettering is white.
(Ref: W17259/DL)

910000 (Taken at Tinsley Yard, 31/5/92)
This vehicle was the first BBA to be built back in October 1975 and is seen here having been recently (judging by the clean paintwork) converted to a BUA for hot steel. Livery is black with yellow warning panels on the upper structure, Flame Red ends, black solebar and bogies, white lettering and red/white logo and fleet name. (Ref: W16997/DL).

offs like the BUA 'hot coffin' steel carrier illustrated above. Even vehicles built as trial prototypes, like the SJA illustrated right, were overtaken by events such as the purchase of the SSA fleet (see Section 15). Others were longer lasting and are covered in Sections 9 to 18, but even some of these had rather brief revenue earning lives such as DC201070 (below right).

Meanwhile the private owner fleet continued to flourish and increase both in overall numbers and diversity of types. Sections 19 to 30 cover these and numerous new designs can be observed, although not surprisingly, relatively few railtank designs. It was still a period of contraction of oil traffic generally and on rail in particular. Both bogie and 4-wheeled railtank chassis were still being revived as box wagons for stone or scrap metal (see example opposite and also Sections 20, 21). Other types continued to be rebuilt or reallocated to traffics they were not initially designed for (see Section 28 in particular for some interesting varieties found on new traffic flows).

Centre. ***361486 (Taken at Tinsley Yard, 31/5/92)***
*This type is fully covered in Section 15, page 38, but this view shows the cleaning door in more detail. Livery is rusty Flame Red body with black solebar and white lettering.
(Ref: W16996/DL).*

Right. ***DC201070 (Taken at Eastleigh Yard, 31/3/92)***
The OTA timber wagons were very prominent in the Southern areas of the U.K. in the late 1980s carrying trees blown down in the great hurricane. After this, some became surplus to requirements and passed to the C.E. for use as sleeper wagons. In this shot, this vehicle is seen still in KRONOSPAN livery (see page 43 for full details). (Ref: W16631/DL)

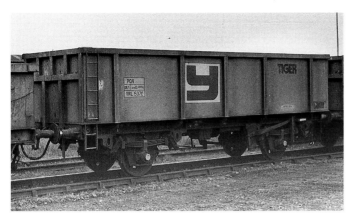

TRL5370 (Taken at Hoo Junction, 31/12/88)
The aggregate POA seen here worked from the Isle of Grain. Livery is light grey body, black solebar and black lettering on white panels. The Yeoman symbol is the usual blue and white and the TIGER symbol yellow and black. (Ref: W14628/DL)

Continental ferry vehicles remained a significant factor in U.K. rail operations and some operated exclusively within that network and rarely, if ever, went on the train ferries. Soon, though, the pattern of this traffic would be changed for ever by the opening of the Channel Tunnel, bogie conflats sweeping away the types seen here for most goods.

The C.E. fleet continued to flourish and, during the review period, fully adopted the recent yellow/Rail Grey livery. The old Olive Green became a familiar sight less and less.

My travels during this period were restricted and I chiefly either stayed in Kent or went looking for specific new designs, especially in 1992. In these later years also, I lacked the opportunities to gain access to official records, or to follow vehicles around the country, as I had done in earlier years and consequently my knowledge in the realms of usage of wagons, especially those privately owned, became less comprehensive. It was at that time, I reviewed the forthcoming changes that would occur with Privatisation and decided not to attempt to follow them, instead I began concentrating on analysing the vast collection of photographs that I had amassed. Ten years on, I know that I made the correct decision.

My efforts since have been to catalogue my collection and to write articles and books. I hope this series will not be my last by any means. I am now looking backwards in time to the period before 1968 and hope, with photographs from both my own collection and from other sources, to provide further historical insights into the wide spectrum of railway freight stock.

My thanks go to all involved in helping me to produce these books and to you the purchasers and readers who I hope share my passion for the subject. Also thanks to the many people who take the time and trouble to write to me with further enquiries, especially those who sometimes have to wait a long time for their answers.

David Larkin,
Sutton , Surrey,
June 2002.

DB996566 (Taken at Reading, 16/5/92)
The Robel crane conversions on the SALMON and STURGEON classes were given the YFA code around 1989 but oddly this one is coded YMA ELK. Livery is yellow and black including lettering. (Ref: W16906/DL)

T.O.P.S. codes

This list gives all the current codes, their meaning and the total quantity extant (in brackets) at the end of 1994 (some of which were introduced after the end of this review period).

BAA	(99) Bogie steel 40'
BBA	(259) Bogie steel 50'
BCA	(55) Bogie Bolster C 30.5t (ex BBA)
BDA	(861) Bogie Bolster D 57t
BEA	(6) Bogie steel carrier
BFA	(89) Bogie Bolster carrier 52t
BGA	(4) Bogie strip coil 13m
BHA	(4) Bogie strip coil 16m
BIA	(5) Bogie strip coil (ex BBA)
BJA	(4) Bogie strip coil 19m
BKA	(3) Bogie steel cradle & hood
BLA	(265) Bogie steel cradle (ex BBA)
BMA	(99) Bogie plate E wide body
BNX	(16) Bogie strip coil K, nylon hood
BOA	(49) Bogie strip coil
BRA	(1) Bogie steel re-bar
BUA	(1) Bogie bolster hot metal carrier
BWA	(13) Bogie bolster coil carrier
BXA	(24) Cradle fitted (Gunshot, ex-BA)
BZA	(118) Cradle fitted (Gunshot, ex-BA)
CAR	(101) Traffic brakevan
CBA	(35) Covhop steel roof

CDA	(139) China clay hopper roller roof
CSA	(99) Fly ash pressure discharge
FBA	(1) Conflat
FNA	(51) Flatrol atomic flask carrier
FPA	(216) Conflat coal/dolphines
HAA	(4841) Coal MGR no canopy
HBA	(381) Coal hopper with canopy
HCA	(113) Coal MGR with canopy
HDA	(32) Coal MGR/hopper no canopy
HEA	(1109) Coal, gravity discharge
HFA	(986) Coal MGR aerodynamic canopy
HSA	(148) Steel scrap, open, two axle
MAA	(5) Mineral, two axle
MEA	(127) Mineral (ex-HE)
MEB	(3) Mineral (ex-HE)
MGA	(1) Mineral (ex-HE) with top cover
MKA	(33) Mineral, open cast coal
OAA	(9) Open 30t/32t
OBA	(50) Open with turnover bolster
OCA	(66) Open with bolster
OIX	(6) Tube, continental RIV
OTA	(165) Timber, 11 stanchions
RRA	(88) Runner wagon two-axle
RRB	(32) Runner wagon two-axle
RRX	(3) Runner wagon two-axle
SDA	(30) Steel bolster two-axle
SEA	(35) Rod coil sideflex hood
SHA	(6) Strip coil (ex-plate)
SJA	(3) Steel scrap open

511009 (Taken at Carlisle Currock, 16/6/92)

In the above list, there is no listing for an FBB but the FBA listed was probably one of these vehicles, designed to carry spirits containers in Scotland and originally vacuum-through piped as well as air-braked. This one is dirty black overall but the buffer beam is red and the lettering is white.(Ref. W17173/DL)

SKA	(53) Rod coil (ex-plate)		**ZCX**	**CHUB** (8) Ballast/spoil open
SPA	(249) Coil/dolophine		**ZDA**	**BASS/ROACH/SQUID** (953) general materials
SSA	(175) Scrap steel open box body		**ZDB**	Plate/Tube general materials
VAA	(83) Vans full length doors, ventilated		**ZEA**	**BREAM** (122) Runner wagon
VBA	(103) Vans full length doors		**ZEB**	**BREAM** (36) Runner wagon
VDA	(98) Vans centre/end cup. doors		**ZEV**	**CATFISH** (490) Ballast hopper, centre chutes
VEA	(31) Van (ex-Vanwide) roller bearings.		**ZEX**	**BREAM** (29) Runner wagon
VGA	(160) Van full length doors		**ZFA**	**GUNNELL** (171) Ballast hopper
YAA	**BRILL** (45) Rail sleeper, ex-BDA		**ZFV**	**DOGFISH** (823) Ballast hopper, centre chutes
YBA	**STURGEON** (213) Rail, sleeper, bolsters		**ZFW**	**DOGFISH** (17) Ballast hopper, centre chutes
YCA	**HALIBUT** (2) Bogie ballast		**ZGA**	**SEAL** (20) General materials
YCV	**TURBOT** (804) Ballast/sleeper dropside		**ZJV**	**MERMAID** (388) Ballast, side tipping
YDA	**SKATE** (32) Seven skip storage		**ZKA**	**LIMPET** (126) Ballast (ex-PGA)
YEA	**PERCH/PORPOISE** (156) LWR wagon		**ZKV**	**BARBEL/ZANDER** (631) Ballast (ex-tippler)
YFA	**SALMON** Borail, lifting gear		**ZUA**	**SHARK** (2) Brake van plough
YGB	**SEACOW/STINGRAY** (515) Ballast hoppers		**ZUB**	**SHARK** (15) Brake van plough
YGH	**SEALION** (218) Ballast hoppers		**ZUV**	**SHARK** (95) Brake van plough
YHA	**WHALE** (87) Ballast hoppers		**ZUW**	**SHARK** (38) Brake van plough
YLA	**MULLET** (80) Borail			
YNA	**SALMON/PARR/EEL** (484) Borail			
YNA	(31) Borail bolster (ex-revenue)			
YPA	**TENCH** (44) Bogie rail, sleeper doors			
YQA	**PARR** (69) Sleeper carrier			
ZAA	**PIKE** (335) Ballast sleeper			
ZBA	**RUDD** (760) Ballast drop sides			
ZBV	**GRAMPUS** (798) Ballast side & end doors			
ZCA	**SEA URCHIN/SEAHARE** (793) Ballast/spoil			
ZCV	**CLAM/PLAICE/TOPE** (1559) Ballast/sleeper wagon with drop sides			

Upon privatisation, the vehicle totals listed above were distributed amongst three freight companies, namely; Loadhaul (formerly Trainload Freight North East), Mainline Freight (formerly Trainload Freight South East) and Transrail (formerly Trainload Freight West). This transfer occurred in April 1994 and I never acquired allocation details (i.e. which vehicle went to which company) for the entire fleet. However, in due course, all three companies were absorbed by English, Welsh and Scottish Railways and operated again as one complete unit. The three-way allocation became reversed and thus irrelevant.

DB991267 (Taken at Woking, 31/3/92)
The ZCV CRAB conversion from the old LAMPREY design remained in use on the S.R. during the review period and was repainted in the new yellow/Rail Grey livery. Solebar here is black with white lettering. (Ref: W16669/DL).

Section 1. Surviving Traditional Wagons (S.R. types)

ADS39524 (Taken at Hoo Junction Yard, 15/3/89)
The S.R. did not produce dedicated wagons for container traffic; the two sizes of vehicle that the company introduced could also be loaded with vehicles. Perhaps this latter characteristic was the reason for the survival of this example. Livery is Olive Green body with black underframe and white lettering. (Ref: W15825/DL).

As mentioned in the introduction, very few traditional vehicles of any sort survived into this review period. Within the ranks of those that did it was something of a surprise to see vehicles built by the Southern Railway - the smallest of the Big Four companies. This could have been because the B.R. Southern Region workshops, responsible for the repairs to such wagons, were quite willing to spend money on converting them to air braking.

The vehicle above, ADS39524, was built as a dual-purpose car-carrying and container wagon and carries the code CONFLAT D. It has been fitted with roller bearings and air through-pipes and was used to carry various railway stores on normal freight services.

DS56117 (opposite upper) was converted in the mid-1960s to operate with YHA WHALE air-braked ballast hoppers (see Vol. 2, pg. 91) and thus survived a lot longer than similar unconverted examples of this standard Southern Railway design.

ADS56296 (opposite centre) was converted a lot earlier to operate on ferry vehicle trains from Dover to Hither Green, south east London. Being bogie vehicles, they gave a much better ride for the guard than four-wheeled brake van designs, as typified by DS56117, and thus their retention was not surprising.

DS62864 (opposite lower) was, however, a surprise retention as most S. R. lines have conductor rails which preclude the use of ballast ploughs. In this case, the plough has been modified and the vehicle fitted with air-pipes.

Opposite Lower. **DS62864 (Taken at Hoo Junction, 4/89)**
It is unclear exactly why the S.R. felt the need to modify any of its plough brake vans but this example has been so modified with a plough that fits over the top of the conductor rail and it has even been repainted. Livery is yellow/Rail Grey body with black solebar and white lettering. (Ref: W16121/DL).

Right. **DS56117 (Taken at Eastleigh, 31/3/92)**
On 1/4/94, there were 55 ZTRs listed. Some of these would have been BR standards, recently modernised, or transferred CARs from the traffic fleet, but it is likely that a fair number were to this design. Livery is faded Olive Green body with black solebar and white lettering. (Ref: W16624/DL)

Centre. **ADS56296 (Taken at Hoo Junction, 4/89)**
These YTX brake vans are not allocated to the C.E. but the C.M. & E.E. and this example was, in fact in use on Channel Tunnel construction traffic. About 11 appear to have been extant on 1/4/94 with various brake types. Livery is Olive Green with yellow ends, black bogies and solebar and white lettering. (Ref: W16122/DL)

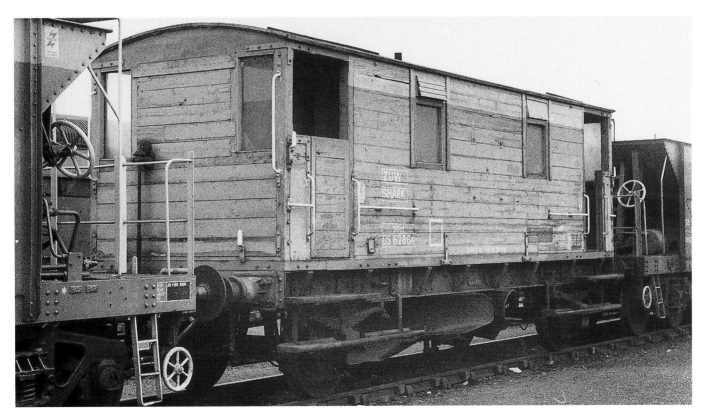

Section 2. Surviving Traditional Wagons (B.R. types)

ADB731597 (Taken at Eastleigh Yard, 31/3/92)
Once they had ceased to be used in revenue earning traffic the vehicles that had been converted to air braking for the B.R. Western Region test train were actively sought by B.R. Southern Region C.M. & E.E. The tube wagon seen here was one such valuable acquisition for use with their stores traffic. Livery is Olive Green body with black underframe and white lettering. (Ref: W16621/DL)

The former opens and vans (opposite upper and centre) which had been used in the B.R. Western Region air-braked test train were fairly early acquisitions for the C.M. & E.E. on the S.R. The tube wagons seen above were acquired rather later, after a spell as oil train barrier wagons in the Stanlow area. The other long wheelbase type - plate wagons - had been converted to conflats for coal containers (see section 16) and when redundant from this traffic were unsuitable as load carriers, having had all bodywork stripped. At least one, though (DB935416) became a ZEB BREAM with the C.E. Full details of the test train fleet are found in Vol. 3, page 38.

Apart from the tube conversions, of which all five seem to be still extant on 1/4/94, very few of the vans or opens appear to have survived, presumably because of their short

wheelbase which would have reduced the maximum operating speed of trains.

Included in this section must be the former tube-style continental ferry opens of Diagram 1/449 (opposite lower). Although fairly elderly, having been built in 1959, they had the same wheelbase as the wagon above and were thus deemed eligible for retention. 16 from an original batch of 20 were listed as extant on 1/4/94.

ADB733228 (Taken at Hoo Junction, 7/12/88)
This is the opposite side of the Diagram 1/449 design and should be compared with the view in Vol. 3, page 41, as the brake lever is very different. Livery is Olive Green body with black solebar and white lettering. (Ref: W14490/DL)

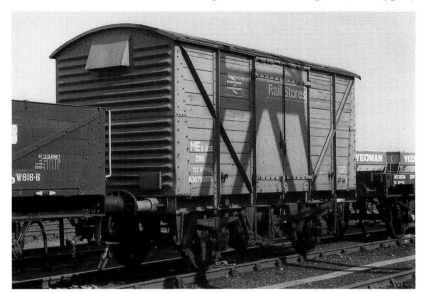

Right. *ADB780575 (Taken at Hoo Junction, 15/3/89)*

The standard B.R. vacuum-braked ventilated van design had long ceased to be seen but the odd one with air pipes could still be found, as seen here. Nine ZRBs were extant on 1/4/94. Livery is Lincoln Green/Rail Grey body, black solebar and white lettering. Unfortunately this vehicle was parked beneath a gantry which cast an inconvenient shadow across the bodyside when it was photographed.(Ref: W15824/DL)

Centre right. *LDE294639 (Taken at Doncaster, 31/5/92)*

Although initially seconded by the S.R., the vehicles of the W.R. test train ranged far and wide, as seen here at Doncaster. Livery is Olive Green body with black solebar and white lettering. (Ref: W17014/DL)

Section 3. Surviving Traditional Wagons (ex-MCV/MSV)

DB388765 (Taken at Bristol East C.E. Depot, 11/3/89)
Unlike the ex-MCVs on the opposite page, the former iron ore tipplers had never been used regularly for coal traffic and had not suffered the corrosion problems which had caused so much rebuilding. Thus they were a useful addition to the C.E., being given the code ZKV BARBEL and receiving full repaints. This one has yet to be done, however, and is in rusty Freight Brown livery with black solebar and white lettering. (Ref: W15609/DL)

The three ZHVs on the opposite page are examples of the fleet of numerous vacuum-braked 16T mineral wagons which were transferred to the C.E. for spoil carrying duties. They were, however, unsatisfactory in one respect over the older highfits that they replaced. Having higher sides and ends meant that a greater quantity of ballast could be loaded, but because this was heavier by volume than coal, especially when wet, it caused the 16T capacity to be exceeded creating difficulties with overloading and braking. To alleviate these problems square or rectangular slots were cut in the sides to indicate the level above which the vehicle was not to be loaded; the spoil, in actual fact, would start falling out if the level was exceeded.

Probably partly due to these problems and partly because the rebuilt bodies were already showing signs of corrosion, they were soon disposed of. Only 98 were extant on 1/4/94,

all being withdrawn from service and stored out of use.

Vacuum-braked MSV wagons (above) were transferred in some numbers to the C.E. department when new privately owned wagons took over the aggregate duties they had been performing. It appears that around 600 were still extant on 1/4/94. Unlike the ex-MCVs, they did not suffer from an overloading problem because they were already rated at 26.5 tonnes. Therefore it was not necessary to modify them in any way.

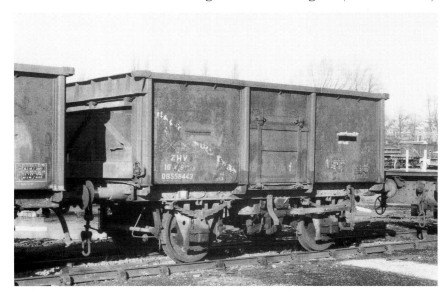

DB558443 (Taken at Northampton, 21/2/89)
This example illustrates the vacuum-braked 16.5T mineral actually built as such, shown by the fitting of eight-shoe clasp brakegear. The cutting of slots was very haphazard. The livery is rusty Freight Brown with black underframe and white lettering. (Ref: W15170/DL)

DB563477 (Taken at Harlow Mill, 20/2/89)
The version illustrated is one of a batch of unfitted wagons which was vacuum-braked in the early 1960s, being fitted at that time with two vacuum cylinders. Once again, the livery of this wagon is rusty Freight Brown with black underframe and white lettering. (Ref: W15083/DL)

DB596035 (Taken at Lidlington, 20/2/89)
Finally, the 10'0" wheelbase type converted from ex-Palbrick chassis is shown, this being rebuilt onto one of the later chassis with eight-shoe clasp brakegear, but without roller bearings. This example is also rusty Freight Brown with black solebar and white lettering. (Ref: W15142/DL)

Section 4. Air Braked Open Wagons (OAA)

100014 (Taken at Hoo Junction Yard, 20/9/89)

The original air-braked open wagon design, the OAA, had long been superseded by newer designs which had more modern running gear and turnover bolsters on the floor. Somewhat surprisingly though, nine were still extant in revenue earning traffic on 1/4/94 and, I believe, others were transferred back from the C.E. department in later years. This example is in patchy Flame Red/ Rail Grey bodywork with black solebar and white lettering. (Ref: W16499/DL)

The OAA class had been built in 1971 and almost all had survived to the beginning of the review period in revenue earning traffic. Quite a few were transferred to the C.E. department as ZDA SQUID wagons and were used for general materials. They were seen on inter-depot engineers trains, which could convey any type of wagon, and they also often formed part of the ancillary stock to ballast trains conveying cranes or track relaying units. A third use was for additional braking force when low-loading wagons such as Flatrols were conveyed to a permanent way renewal site. These latter did not have operational air brakes, only through connecting pipes.

Some vehicles, such as DC100093 (opposite centre), received Sector livery before transfer to the C.E. Others, such as DC100065 (opposite top), received a special C.E. livery after transfer to keep them on the inter-depot traffic.

Finally, there was one variant that was given higher ends and fitted with internal blue nylon straps to hold down pallets of roof tiles. These were used from Stirling and Rugby along with bogie PO wagons and painted in the livery of Redland Ltd. Numbers I have been able to identify are 100016/34/ 42/61/3/77/84/6. This variation is illustrated by DC100077 (opposite lower).

Opposite Centre. **DC100093 (Taken at Eastleigh, 31/3/92)**

This OAA has received the full Sector livery of dark grey sides/ yellow ends before transfer to the C.E. but has had the symbol overpainted. The lettering is FOR R.C.E.(S.R.) INTER DEPOT USE ONLY. (Ref: W16623/DL)

Opposite Lower. **DC100077 (Taken at Woking, 31/3/92)**

The vehicles that had been in the REDLAND traffic carried that company's distinctive pale green livery and this fact, plus the obvious modifications picked them out. Main lettering here is white on black with NO LOOSE SHUNTING in black. The Fox symbol is black and white and the other lettering (as both above) is white. (Ref: W16691/DL)

Right. **DC100065 (Taken at Woking, 31/3/92)**
This example has been repainted in the full yellow/ light grey C.E. livery but, as well as the lettering noted on the wagon below, it also carries the name CIVIL LINK in light grey on the yellow band. (Ref: W16689/DL)

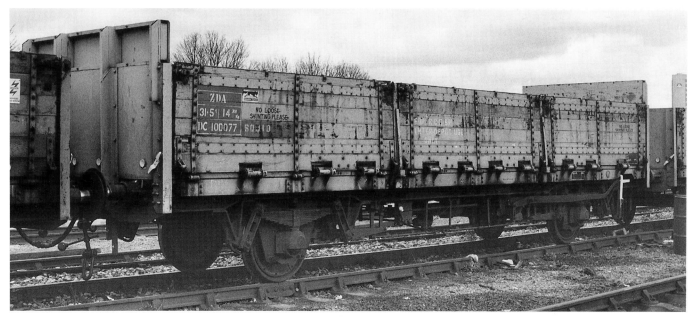

Section 5. Air Braked Open Wagons (OBA and OCA)

110688 (Taken at Dumfries, 25/10/88)

There was not all that much genuine general merchandise traffic to be conveyed at the start of the review period and I have the suspicion that the OBAs seen here were actually in timber traffic, there being insufficient OTAs available. The high ends of the OBA would be useful for this traffic and the floor had turnover bolsters to allow unloading by fork lift truck if necessary, or perhaps allowing securing chains to be passed under the logs. Livery is a rather faded Flame Red/Rail Grey with black solebar and white lettering. (Ref: W14200/DL)

Only 50 OBAs were still in revenue earning service on 1/4/94, the majority allocated to Loadhaul. In 1991, known numbers had been 110533/6/9/44/6 – 9/51/2/4 – 61/3 – 6/9/71/3 – 5/7/80/1/3/5/9/90/2 – 5/7/9, 110600/5 – 7/10/6/7/23/7/8/31/5/7 – 9/41/3 – 6/8/9/55/6/8/9/64/7/8/70 – 3/6 – 8/80 – 4/6 – 8/90 – 4/6/7, 110700/2/4 – 6/8/10 – 6/20 – 4/6 – 9/31 – 4/8 – 41/3/8/50/2/3/5/6/8/9/61/2/5 – 73/5/8/81/3/4/7/8/90 – 2/4/7/8, 110800.

Most of the remainder of unmodified vehicles seem to have become ZDA BASS wagons (as opposite top).

The OBA featured in a number of conversions, including the RRA (see Section 12) and the PLASMOR variant (see Section 37).

Of the 66 OCAs extant on 1/4/94, the majority were with Transrail. Known numbers in 1991 were 112159/63/4/9/71 – 4/6/9/81/91 – 3/5/7 – 9, 112200 – 3/5/6/9/11/3 – 5/8/

9/21/2/4/7 – 30/2/3/8/40/4/5/9/50/2/4/6/8 – 62/5/70/73/4/7/9/84/5/7/93/5/7/8, 112300/5 – 7/9/11/5/20/1/5/6/31/5/7/44/6/8/50/4/6/7/9 – 63/7/8/73 – 5/7/9/90/2/3/5/7/8.

Quite a few of these also went to the C.E. fleet (see opposite lower). Conversions of note are the OTA (see section 17) and the ZCA Seahorse (see section 41).

Opposite Lower. ***112230 (Taken at Carlisle, 16/6/92)***
The OCA seen here is actually lettered TO WORK BETWEEN CARLISLE CURROCK 08191 AND St. BLAZEY 85221, which suggests inter-depot traffic for the C & W dept. Livery of dark grey sides and yellow ends is applied with black solebar, white lettering and red/yellow sector symbol. The Fox symbol is black and white. (Ref: W17171/DL)

KDC110588 (Taken at Woking, 31/3/92)
The former OBA seen here has recently been passed to the S & T department to transport their stores around between depots. Livery here is yellow/Flame Red body with black solebar and white lettering on black panel. The SATLINK logo is black. (Ref: W16673/DL)

Right. **112249 (Taken at Hoo Junction, 8/89)**
The OCA design was really an SPA with higher sides and it was not surprising for similar loads to be carried, as seen here loaded with steel wire coils. Livery is Flame Red with black solebar and white lettering. (Ref: W16441/DL)

Section 6. Air Braked Vans (VAA, VBA, VDA)

200148 (Taken at Doncaster, 31/5/92)
Even twenty years after their construction and the introduction of T.O.P.S. codes, the anomaly over the VAA and VBA coding was still evident, this example being coded VAA (i.e. with vent) when it plainly does not have one. Sector livery is applied with Dark Grey sides, yellow ends, black solebar and white lettering. The partially obliterated sector symbol is red/yellow. (Ref: W17008/DL)

The traditional early air-braked vans were still listed in 1992, but those I saw at Doncaster appeard to be stored out of use, perhaps for rebuilding. Of the 83 VAAs extant (see above) on 1/4/94, most went to Transrail.

There were rather more VBAs (opposite upper) - 103, and most of these were allocated to Loadhaul.

The VCA was eliminated in revenue earning traffic some time previously, leaving the only other variant, the VDA (opposite centre and lower) in use. In 1/4/94 there were 98 of these and again most of them were with Loadhaul.

The VCA however was used for a number of conversions, including the PLASMOR POAs (see Section 37) and were given new numbers.

VDA conversions had featured quite early, as RRA runner wagons, but all these were now recoded as ZEA BREAM wagons. Of more significance were those rebuilt as OTA timber wagons (see Section 17).

When introduced in the early 1970s, these vans represented a major advance in British wagon design when set alongside to the traditional 10' 0" wheelbase designs (see ADB780575 on page 13). However, they were really only comparable with European practice dating from the late 1950s and early 1960s periods.

Thus they were phased out relatively quickly from BR van traffic, partly by the VGA type covered in Section 7, but chiefly by the four-wheeled and bogie Private Owner ferry vans seen in Sections 33 to 35.

Above. ***200253 (Taken at Cardiff Tidal, 6/6/92)***
If past precedent is anything to go by, the van seen here at Cardiff is carrying tinplate. Sector livery is present with weathered dark grey sides and yellow ends, black solebar, and white lettering. Sector symbol is red/yellow and the Fox symbol black and white. (Ref: W17051/DL)

Centre. ***200706 (Taken at Doncaster, 31/5/92)***
The VDA was the most numerous of the original air-braked vans and was still to be seen in significant numbers in 1992. This example is a prototype for Sector livery. Sides are Rail Grey and ends yellow, solebar and lettering black. The red/yellow sector symbol is only on one side and the Fox symbol is black and white. (Ref: W17006/DL)

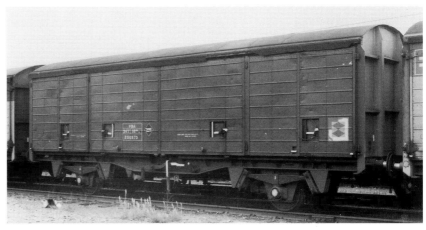

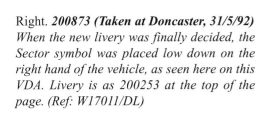

Right. ***200873 (Taken at Doncaster, 31/5/92)***
When the new livery was finally decided, the Sector symbol was placed low down on the right hand of the vehicle, as seen here on this VDA. Livery is as 200253 at the top of the page. (Ref: W17011/DL)

Section 7. Air Braked Vans (VEA and VGA)

230469 (Taken at Doncaster, 31/5/92)

I believe that the reasoning behind the yellow painted ends of vehicles in Sector livery was for Health and Safety purposes to warn staff on the tracks; for example, in shunting manoeuvres, the yellow panels of locomotives would be obscured by vehicles being propelled. However, this feature was rather lost on the VEA, since the corrugated ends soon filled with grime, dulling the paintwork. This class was the last still running with this once common feature. Livery is Dark Grey with yellow ends, black solebar and white lettering. The sector symbol and the Fox symbol are the usual colours. (Ref: W17017/DL)

Only 35 VEAs were extant on 1/4/94 and the Transrail fleet had most of them. They had always been associated with military traffic (see opposite upper) and perhaps this was beginning to dwindle too.

The VGA emulated contemporary European designs (see Section 33) and were by no means outdated during the review period. 160 were listed with Transrail on 1/4/94, and apart from two early withdrawals, the remainder are thought to have been in the Railfreight Distribution fleet, which was at this time separate from the other freight companies.

These two designs (i.e. the VGA as new, and the VEA as a rebuild) seem to have been the last traditional general merchandise vans built for the national system and it is interesting to pause to compare and contrast totals of such types through the decades. Only 2300 air-braked vans,

including the VEA rebuilds, were constructed between 1969 and 1983. By comparison, well over 35,000 traditional 10' 0" wheelbase general merchandise vans (including pallet vans and Vanwides) were built between 1949 and 1962 by British Railways.

Although load capacities and utilisation had increased of course, the statistics did in fact reflect the national trend of such traffic being transferred from rail to road. A case of history repeating itself perhaps, since the LMS alone had produced almost 43,000 such vans between 1924 and 1947.

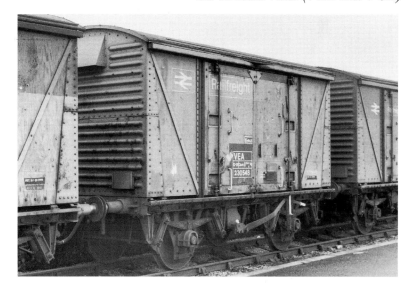

230548 (Taken at Ludgershall, 9/3/89)
By this review period the survival of a short wheelbase 12T van type was clearly something of an anachronism. The basis of the design can be traced back to Victorian times, so how and why had this quaint wagon shape stood the test of time? Principally it was down to the many rail served M.o.D. depots that contained very sharp curves. The 20' 9" wheelbase standard air-braked vans were too long to negotiate them, hence the 10' 0" wheelbase Vanwide was upgraded with air brakes and reclassified to VEA for this traffic. This example is in Flame Red/Rail Grey livery with white lettering and black and white Fox symbol. It provides an interesting comparison with that illustrated in volume 3, page 9. (Ref: W15493/DL).

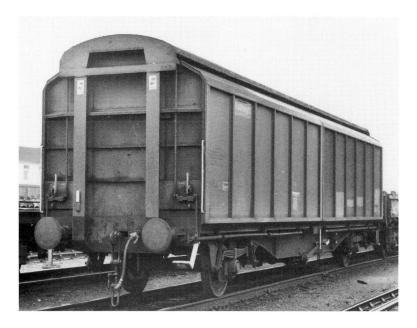

210463 (Taken at Southampton, 10/3/89)
When new, the shiny natural metal sides and Flame Red ends of the VGA were really eyecatching, but in this shot, the vehicle is decidedly grubby and the colourful livery less marked. The RAILFREIGHT symbol is white on red and the Fox symbol black and white. A small number of vans originally appeared with a plate to carry the Railfreight and double arrow symbol, but the vast majority of the fleet were devoid of this fitment.
(Ref: W15502/DL)

210644 (Taken at Carlisle, 16/6/92)
When the VGAs were repainted into Sector livery, I believe that the door sides were cleaned back to the natural metal finish, rather than painted silver. Ends are now yellow and the solebar black. The wagon number is white on black, the Sector symbol red/yellow and Fox symbol black and white. Door opening instruction panels are black on white.
(Ref: W17169/DL)

Section 8. Bogie Steel Wagons (Traditional)

B949508 (Taken at Hamworthy, 13/3/89)
The BNX bogie coil wagons first appeared in the 1960s and, due to them being fitted with Westinghouse brakes for continental duties during their career, they were able to continue on the same duties into the air-braked era. Bodywork is Freight Brown with grey nylon hoods, bogies are black and lettering white. (Ref: W15805/DL)

Traditional bogie steel carrying wagons were represented by a number of types during the review period.

The BNX bogie strip coil wagons (above), fitted with Westinghouse brakes, continued in use, often operating with the Powell Duffryn wagons seen in Section 38. 16 were extant on 1/4/94 and all were allocated to Loadhaul.

The BVW class (opposite upper) were also for strip coil but to a different design because of the requirements of the original user. 21 of these were still extant on 1/4/94 but all were withdrawn and stored out of use. Numbers for these were B949050 to B949089.

Although two prototype BCAs had been produced in the 1970s to test conversion of unfitted Bogie Bolster Cs with air-brakes, this programme had not been continued. However, certain vacuum-braked examples were given air-pipes and coded BCW (opposite centre). Sample numbers

for these were B923103, B923217, B924424, B924562, B924612 and B924798. Only three withdrawn vehicles were extant on 1/4/94.

Similarly, vacuum-braked Bogie Bolster Ds were also given air-pipes and coded BDW and, once again, only three withdrawn vehicles survived to 1/4/94. Sample numbers for these were B927800/14/27/33/41/52/66/74/82/90, B927901/13/26/35/44/59/65/74/88/90, B928003/11/23/36/40/55/61/74/85/98, B928102/11/25/34/42/56/67/70/88/94.

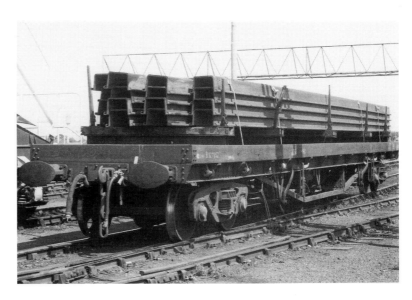

Above. **B949054 *(Taken at Swindon, 13/3/89)***
The BVW class were retained because they were custom built strip coil wagons but were less useful in air-braked trains, being air-piped only. Livery is basically rusty brown with shiny grey nylon sheets. Any visible lettering is white. (Ref: W15733/DL)

Centre. **B924612 *(Taken at Hoo Junction, 7/89)***
The BCW conversions were all selected from the BCV batches that had Gloucester bogies. Other features were the removal of chains and replacement by blue nylon straps. Livery is Flame Red body, black solebar and bogies and white lettering. (Ref: W16331/DL)

Right. **B927952 *(Taken at Hoo Junction, 5/89)***
The BDW conversions were also restricted to batches with Gloucester bogies, again blue nylon straps were provided. The load of both this vehicle and the BCW (above) is 'U' channel piling for the Channel Tunnel construction site. This example does not appear to have been painted for a very long time and is thus very rusty, with any lettering in white. (Ref: W16163/DL)

Section 9. Air Braked Steel Wagons (SPA and variants)

460339 (Taken at Cardiff, 6/6/92)
As there was very little steel plate traffic to be conveyed during the review period, most SPAs seen loaded were carrying rod coil as seen here and operating with the specialist conversions. Livery is faded Flame Red with black solebar and white lettering. The Double Arrow and RAILFREIGHT symbols are the usual white on red, and the CARDIFF RODMILL logo is a combination of red, black, blue and white. (Ref: W17046/DL)

The SPA class was built in significant numbers, though traffic did not come up to original expectations and they were steadily reduced, either by conversion or transfer to the C.E. as ZAA PIKE.

249 were still listed as SPA on 1/4/94, Transrail having the largest fleet, followed by Loadhaul, then Mainline. They are also noted as carrying dolophine, which I believe is a brand name for a derivative of the mineral dolomite.

53 vehicles represented the SKA conversion (opposite upper) and the bulk of these were with Mainline. Sample numbers are 460362, 460430, 460596, 460728 and 460849.

35 wagons were listed as SEA conversions (opposite centre) and these were all with Mainline. Sample numbers are 460385, 460454, 460546, 460608, 460760 and 460832.

30 wagons were noted as SDA conversions (opposite lower) and Loadhaul had all of these. Sample numbers are 460612, 460709, 460822, 460973 and 461076.

One other conversion, not illustrated, was the SHA which

was formerly coded KTA and carried three rolls of strip coil 'eye-to-sky'. The original body sides were retained and each roll was sheeted for protection. Loadhaul had all six of these, sample numbers are 460707/22/6/9/61/81/92/9, 460811/ 42. The remaining unconverted wagons had been transferred to the C.E. and are covered in Section 41.

Opposite Top. *460430 (Taken at Cardiff, 6/6/92)*
The SKA conversion followed a pattern set in the mid-1960s for this type of load (see Vol. 2, pg. 59) but this version was not fitted with high ends. There is now very little paintwork visible and even the sides are unpainted. Any lettering is white. (Ref: W17050/DL).

Opposite Lower. *460822 (Taken at Rotherham, 22/10/88)*
The reappearance of the double bolster type in the air-braked fleet was something of a surprise but undoubtedly it was for a specific traffic in the Rotherham area. Livery on this SDA is Flame Red ends, black solebar and white lettering. (Ref: W14113/DL).

Right. **460608 *(Taken at Cardiff, 6/6/92)***
The SEA conversions were much more colourful. Presumably there was a need for bright steel rod, requiring the load to be kept dry in transit. Hence the fitting of the nylon hood which is dark blue with standard logos and markings. The sides and ends are Flame Red and solebar black. Lettering is white.
(Ref: W17048/DL).

Section 10. Air Braked Bogie Steel Wagons (1)

900187 (Taken at Carlisle Citadel, 16/6/92)
Photographs of the BAA in totally original condition during the review period (and indeed the previous one) are hard to come by, even this example has modified ends from an early duty as a strip coil wagon. The weathered livery has Flame Red ends, black solebar and bogies and white lettering. Note the number on the end. (Ref: W17182/DL)

99 BAAs are listed as being extant on 1/4/94, the larger proportion of the fleet being with Loadhaul, the remainder with Transrail.

Most of this fleet were coil carriers of one sort or another. There were the 'Gunshot' types, so-called because the coils were loaded longitudinally and were supposed to resemble a gun barrel, whilst other types carried coil transversely on special supporting cradles.

The gunshot types were coded BYA (opposite upper) but this code was not in use on 1/4/94. Known numbers were 900007/10/5/23/4/6/32/6/54/5/70, 900157/96, 900213/86. 118 were listed as BZA (opposite centre) on 1/4/94 and all were with Loadhaul. Sample numbers are; 900001/33/56/92, 900113/40/62/85, 900205/40/73, 900303.

49 BOA conversions of the former XVA trestle wagon (see Vol. 3, pg. 53) were extant on 1/4/94, but they were stored out of service by Loadhaul. Known numbers are; 990003/8/15/6/33.

Opposite Top. **900205 (Taken at Cardiff, 6/6/92)**
The 'Gunshot' name for this class was not all that appropriate because invariably the coils had gaps between them for load distribution. This example is in Sector livery with yellow ends, black solebar and lettering and the appropriate sector symbol. (Ref: W5231/DL)

Opposite Centre. **900196 (Taken at Cardiff, 6/6/92)**
Although a BZA, this wagon is carrying the painted code BAA, illustrating the difficulties in pinning the various conversions down. In 1992, it was listed on T.O.P.S. as a BYA, a code which was subsequently dropped. Livery is Flame Red and black with white lettering. (Ref: W17069/DL)

Opposite Lower. **990033 (Taken at Cardiff Tidal, 6/6/92)**
The former XVA fleet had a somewhat tenuous early career, being fairly soon converted to RRA runner wagons by having the trestle equipment removed. Here we see the strip coil variant. Livery is Flame Red and black with white lettering. (Ref: W17065/DL)

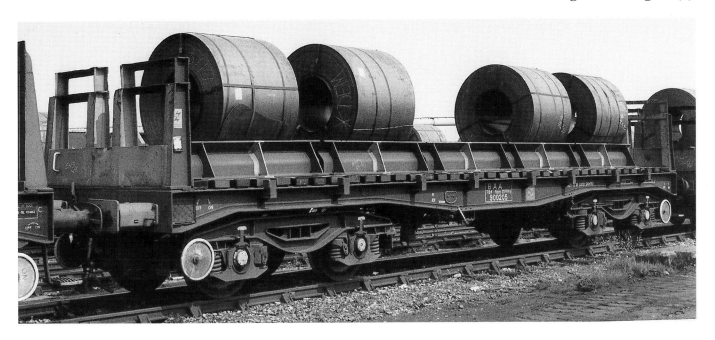

Section 11. Air Braked Bogie Steel (2)

950191 (Taken at Dumfries, 25/10/88)
This BTA appears to have been a somewhat short lived conversion of the basic BDA. Its presence at Dumfries suggests timber traffic, as does the code, but it could have been carrying gas pipeline sections. Livery is Flame Red ends, Rail Grey sides, black solebar and bogies and white lettering, RAILFREIGHT on red. (Ref: W14204/DL)

The BDA conversions of the old unfitted BDO were still around in some numbers during the review period, only relatively few being transferred to the C.E. as YAA BRILL. 861 vehicles were extant on 1/4/94, Loadhaul having the majority, followed by Transrail, whilst Mainline had only 34. However, various conversions occurred with certain vehicles.

The BTA conversion illustrated above appears to have been very short lived, with none existing on 1/4/94. Known numbers are 950017, 950123/91, 950839.

The BFA conversions were working with the SDA fleet (see Section 9) and, like them, the 89 remaining examples on 1/4/94 were used by Loadhaul. Sample numbers are as follows; 950370, 950514, 950621, 950700, 950862, 950930 and 951003.

The BMA conversions were taken from both BDAs and BPAs and are listed for carrying plates, although both

examples seen here are carrying similar loads to the BFAs. Sample numbers for the former BDAs are 950003, 950101, 950203, 950523, 950607, 950745 and 950833. Sample numbers for those converted from former BPAs are 965029, 965032, 965046, 965050, 965061 and 965077. On 1/4/94 they were split between Loadhaul and Transrail, the former having the slightly higher quantity.

It is interesting to note the longevity of this design. Although first introduced by the LNER in the late 1930s, it was never wholly superseded by more modern designs, such as that illustrated in Section 10, but was upgraded in respect of brakes and bogies.

Right. **950621 (Taken at Rotherham, 22/10/88)**
Unlike the SDA conversions in Section 9, the BFA only required taller stanchions to be reclassified with the new code and be kept on dedicated traffic. Livery is Flame Red body, black solebar and bogies and white lettering. (Ref: W14107/DL)

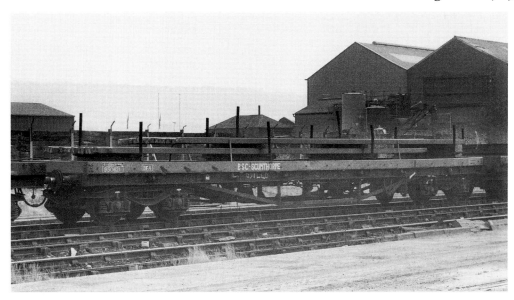

Centre. **950012 (Taken at Grimsby, 29/5/92)**
The BMA conversion on the BDA was much more radical and involved new ends and the replacement of the bolsters with a BAA/BBA type floor. Livery involved Flame Red ends, black solebar and bogies and white lettering. (Ref: W16919/DL)

Below. **965059 (Taken at Grimsby, 29/5/92)**
Once the BMA conversion had been carried out, it was only possible to differentiate the former BPAs from the more numerous former BDAs by their numbers, since new the code was the same. The livery is exactly the same as above. (Ref: W16916/DL)

Section 12. Air Braked Runner Wagons

B787108 (Taken at Cardiff Tidal, 6/6/92)
The need for runner wagons is well illustrated in this view. The RRX is marshalled between two BDAs which are both loaded with reinforcing rod longer than the bogie wagon. The floor of the runner is unpainted and the remainder is black with red buffer beams and white lettering. (Ref: W17072/DL)

Only three RRX runners converted from ferry vans were listed on 1/4/94. In 1983, the fleet consisted of 34 and known numbers are GB787108, GB787116, GB787188 and GB787324. All were fitted with Bruninghaus springs.

The STEEL AB class (SAA and SAB) had long featured in the runner wagon fleet and this was now formerly recorded. The RRBs (opposite upper) had vacuum-pipes and were numbered 400000 – 3/5/6/8 – 16/8 – 35/7 – 42/4/5. Those coded RRA were 400173, 400236/65/72/7/83. 32 RRBs were extant on 1/4/94, all with Loadhaul.

The RRA illustrated opposite centre was converted from an OBA and this fleet was numbered 110538/40/2/53/67/70/2/6, 110601 – 3/13/22/32/4/40/75/9/95/8/9, 110707/9/17/35/6/42/4/5/7/9/51/64/74/6/9/85/9/96. A total of 88 RRAs were listed on 1/4/94, the majority being with Loadhaul and a few with Transrail.

B787403 (opposite lower) was converted from the old fleet of pallet vans allocated to Ford traffic and known numbers are B787400, B787403, B787419, B787426, B787431 B787435, B787460 and B787474. These were coded RRB but, not having been re-sprung, are not thought to be part of the above total.

Right. **400032 *(Taken at Cardiff, 6/6/92)***

The former STEEL AB wagons were in largely unmodified condition except for the removal of the turnover bolsters and the hinged stanchions on the sides. This example is painted Rail Grey with red buffer beam, black solebar and white lettering. (Ref: W17077/DL)

Centre. ***110570 (Taken at Cardiff, 6/6/92)***

The OBA conversion to RRA involved a new metal mesh floor and small angled sides, the purpose of which is unclear! These latter were painted Freight Brown, solebar was black and lettering white. (Ref: W17070/DL)

Below. **B787403 *(Taken at Hoo Junction Yard, 4/89)***

To add a bit of weight to the converted runner wagon, scrap rail was fixed to the floor, as in the case of these vehicles. This example is grubby overall but some wagons of this type have been recorded with red buffer beams. (Ref: W16102/DL)

Section 13. Air Braked Hoppers (HAA and variations)

356533 (Taken at Cardiff Tidal, 6/6/92)
The vast majority of the MGR fleet at this time were still of the HAA type as this example illustrates. Liveries however had changed with Sectorisation and this one has a weathered natural metal body, yellow framing, black solebar and white lettering on black panels. The coal sector symbol is black and yellow and the other names and symbols are black and white. (Ref: W17055/DL).

The second prototype HAA had been fitted with a top canopy and a small fleet so built operated in Scotland for many years. However, the story goes that, following a complaint about washing being dirtied by dust blown from an uncovered load, such as seen above, canopies began to be fitted to many more vehicles. Because of the canopy issue, the HAA fleet underwent changes and re-codings in 1992, though even by 1/4/94, the bulk of the fleet were still HAAs; a total of 4841 in fact. Loadhaul took the biggest quantity but Mainline and Transrail both took over 1000.

Of the canopied variants, the biggest batch of the 381 HBA type (not illustrated) went to Mainline, with equal proportions for Loadhaul and Transrail. Transrail received almost all of the 113 HCA type (opposite upper) and all of the HDA 60 mph variant. Finally, there were nearly 1000 of an HFA variant (not illustrated) which was fitted with an aerodynamic canopy, these were divided roughly equally between the three freight companies.

The CBA fleet (opposite centre) totalled 35 on 1/4/94 and these all went to Transrail.

The CDA fleet (opposite lower) was a new addition in this review period. After the successful conversion of a 'cleaned' HAA in 1986, BREL Doncaster produced Lot 4062 during 1987/88. These were completely new vehicles and numbered 375000 to 375123. By 1991, three design codes (CD 001A, CD 002A and CD 002B) are quoted for these vehicles but I have not yet determined what the differences were.

Further vehicles were added to the fleet in 1989. These were conversions from HAAs, carried out by RFS Doncaster, and were given numbers 375124 to 375137. These may have included the original 1986 conversion. The design code for these was CD 001B. The whole fleet went to Transrail on 1/4/94.

351638 (Taken at Burton-on-Trent, 24/7/92)
As would be expected, the fitting of the canopies appears to have been carried out at dedicated MGR Carriage & Wagon depots, like the one at Burton. This must have been an early example as the whole wagon appears uniformly weathered. The framing is Freight Brown.(Ref: W17280/DL)

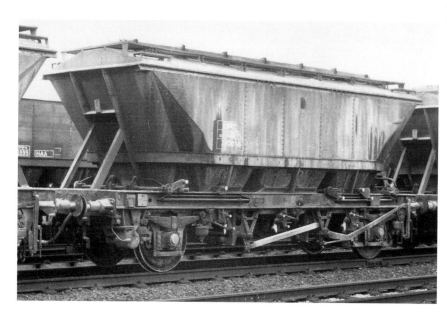

250038 (Taken at Burton-on-Trent, 22/2/89)
The CBA class, being very similar to HAAs, were also serviced at Burton. This lime stained example also had Freight Brown framing with black solebar and white lettering on a black panel. Comparison with a similar vehicle in Vol. 2, pg. 85 shows that they changed very little during their lives. (Ref: W15283/DL)

375116 (Taken at Par, 24/6/92)
The CDA class took over from the UCV Clay Hood wagons (see Vol. 3, pg. 8) and operated only within the Cornwall china clay circuit. When new, they were rather colourful with blue ECC symbol and bracing and red hood but, as can be seen here, they got covered in white clay dust very quickly. (Ref: W17242/DL)

Section 14. Air Braked Hoppers (HEA and derivatives)

361994 (Taken at Bow Goods, East London, 19/2/89)
The HBA hopper (see Vol. 2., page 85) had been specifically designed to carry domestic coal rather than industrial coal, which was catered for by the HAA fleet. By now all were coded as HEAs to reflect the change in springing; this illustration, however, shows one of the last ones built which, unlike the majority of the class, were fitted with Bruninghaus springs from new. The livery seen here is the Speedlink Flame Red/Rail Grey, only a couple apparently ever receiving the dark grey Sector livery. The size of the double arrow symbol and the RAILFREIGHT fleet name varied considerably amongst these wagons. (Ref: W14996/DL)

HEA domestic coal hoppers (above) in original condition numbered 1109 on 1/4/94, mostly allocated to Transrail but sizeable quantities with both Loadhaul and Mainline. Many of the type were converted and fitted with box bodies during the review period.

One such conversion was the HSA scrap carrier, illustrated opposite, 148 were extant on 1/4/94 and most went to Loadhaul. Mainline had 40 but they were all in store at that time. Sample numbers are 360036, 360122, 360215, 360353, 360454, 360511, 360616, 360729, 360840, 360914, 361061, 361187, 361278, 361312, 361434, 361538, 361661, 361758, 361859 and 361998.

127 MEA conversions (opposite upper) were listed on 1/4/94 and the fleet was split up fairly evenly between the three companies. Converted from 1990 onwards, these vehicles were numbered 391000 to 391126.

Very similar to the MEA, were the MAA conversions (opposite centre), but these were rebuilt from HAA hoppers. There were only 5 vehicles, numbered 392000 to 392004, and all went to Transrail on 1/4/94.

It is pertinent to reflect that the time honoured method of discharging coal loads through bottom doors into a pit beneath the track was soon to be relegated to history. The development of modern hydraulic grab machines meant that unloading could now easily be undertaken almost anywhere and obviated the need for expensive pit and conveyor infrastructure. The same principle also being applied to aggregate traffic resulted in the gradual elimination of many hopper wagon types in favour of box bodies as the review period drew to a close.

Above. **391018 *(Taken at Barry, 6/6/92)***
The MEA conversion took the place of the MDO mineral wagons on the Swansea export coal traffic (see Vol. 2, pg. 16). The sides were dark grey, ends were yellow and solebar black. Lettering is white and sector symbol yellow and black.
(Ref: W17044/DL)

Centre. **392000 *(Taken at Swansea, 23/6/92)***
The trial fleet of new box-bodied coal wagons for the traffic mentioned above also included some HAA conversions, which were given vacuum pipes. When the pipes were later removed, the TOPS code was amended and the vehicles renumbered, note the fresh patches of paint in the number panel. Livery is as above. (Ref: W17207/DL)

Right. **360036 *(Taken at Tinsley Yard, 31/5/92)***
One of the least obvious conversions of the HEA hopper wagon was to the HSA scrap wagon shown here. Basically the doors were secured in the shut position as all discharge was by grab or electromagnet from above. The blue on white (St Andrews) cross identifies the wagon as being formerly in a Scottish Speedlink Coal pool. Livery here is rusty Freight Brown with white lettering. (Ref: W16998/DL)

Section 15. Air Braked Scrap Wagons

360040 (Taken at Tinsley Yard, 31/5/92)
The SJA scrap wagon was very similar to the MEA conversion seen on the previous page, having an access door at the left hand of each side. This feature can be more easily seen on page 5. Livery is Flame Red with black solebar and white lettering. (Ref: W16995/DL)

After producing the MFA scrap wagon (see Vol. 3, pg. 56) B.R. did not produce any similar wagons until the SJA conversions shown above. The three original conversions, numbered 360040, 360761 and 361486, were not followed by any others, though they were still listed on 1/4/94 with Loadhaul.

Instead, in 1990 B.R. decided to purchase former privately owned stock from the Railease fleet featured in Vol. 3, pg. 57. Renumbering followed and the prototype RLS5900 became 470100, with RLS5000 to RLS5099 becoming 470000 to 470099 (example illustrated opposite upper) and RLS5901 to RLS5980 becoming 470101 to 470180 (examples illustrated opposite centre and opposite lower).

The latter batch involves three design codes, viz. 470101 to 470120 (SS 001B), 470121 to 470150 (SS 001C) and 470151 to 470180 (SS 001D).

All these acquisitions were coded SSA and the total of 175 that were still existing on 1/4/94 were split between Loadhaul and Transrail, with Loadhaul having a slightly higher quantity.

Subsequent development of the scrap carrying fleet has been rather interesting. As noted in Section 20, the Private Owner wagons shown here were almost immediately replaced by further four-wheeled examples. The trend however, has been for more bogie wagons, similar to the bogie aggregate vehicles in section 21, and this, I believe, also became EWS policy.

Above. **470084 (Taken at Tinsley, 31/5/92)**
All the SSAs had slight body detail differences, this example, one of the batch built on the ex-BSRV hopper chassis (see RLS5026 in Vol. 3, pg. 57) has a ladder but no access door. The original blue side/yellow end livery is still carried but now in a very worn condition. (Ref: W16989/DL)

Centre. **470103 (Taken at Tinsley, 31/5/92)**
In this version, there is no ladder but there is a prominent access door. The bodywork has suffered some considerable distress in traffic; compare with its sister vehicle in original condition - RLS5901, Vol. 3, pg. 57. The vehicle has a lever operated brake rather than a hand wheel. Livery is as above. (Ref: W16990/DL)

Right. **470130 (Taken at Tinsley, 31/5/92)**
This version is an example of design code SS 001C. It is very similar to the vehicle shown at the top of this page, although the hand brake is a lever operated version. Livery is as above. (Ref: W16986/DL)

Section 16. Air Braked Conflat Wagons

400227 (Taken at Gartcosh, 26/10/88)
An example of an FPA flat, No. 400227, is seen here without a container. Livery is black with red buffer beam and white lettering. When compared with the old traditional Conflats, which required chains to keep the containers secured on the wagons, the standard I.S.O. design is seen to be much more efficient. Short pegs or guides at each corner position the container on the wagon underframe which is then secured with steel pins, features which can be seen more clearly on the wagon to the right of 400227. (Ref: W14219/DL)

Coal traffic in containers dates back to the very early days of railways in the U.K. There was something of a revival in Central Scotland in the 1980s and the first wagons used were the plate wagons from the W.R. air-braked test train.

These were superseded by STEEL AB (SAA) conversions from the mid 1980s, as seen in this section. Numbers were 400046/7/9/51/4/5/7/9/60/2 – 6/8/9/71/2/5 – 9/81/2/5/6/8 – 91/3 – 5/7 – 9, 400101 – 5/9/10/2 – 9/21/3 – 6/9/31/2/4 – 41/3/4/6 – 50/2 – 67/9/71/4 – 9/82 – 8/90/2 – 6/9, 400200 – 12/4 – 8/20 – 4/6 – 9/31 – 5/7 – 40/ 2/3/6 – 50/2 – 4/6 – 60/2 – 4/7 – 71/3/4/8 – 82/5/6/8 – 95/9.

The fleet was later supplemented by FPA conversions from VCA van chassis (opposite lower). These were numbered 200325/7/8/30/1/4/7/42/4/6/8/9/51/2/4/9/61/3/6/85, 200459/65, 200501/20.

A total of 216 FPAs were extant on 1/4/94 and all had been transferred to Transrail.

One company which operated the containers for several years was Russell, carrying coal from South Yorkshire to Central Scotland and Inverness. The containers themselves did have detail differences as seen opposite. Other uses were for the carriage of road salt and for British Sugar traffic.

Opposite Top. **400183 (Taken at Mossend, 26/10/88)**
This FPA carries an early RUSSELL container with end doors and a different pattern of ribs on the sides. Livery for the container is orange with white lettering on purple panels. The wagon flat is now in overall dirty black with white lettering. (Ref: W14243/DL)

Opposite Centre. **400156 (Taken at West Drayton, 2/6/92)**
This combination is seen at another destination recorded for this type, West Drayton. In this case, the container has a simpler pattern of side ribbing and is painted silver with white lettering on black. The FPA is black with red buffer beam and white lettering. (Ref: W17027/DL)

Right. *200342 (Taken at West Drayton, 2/6/92)*

The FPAs converted from VCAs are indistinguishable from those from the SAAs (they had exactly the same chassis anyway). Only the number identifies the original source. Both container and wagon livery are exactly as above, however, there are some subtle differences to note between the containers.
(Ref: W17032/DL)

Section 17. Air Braked Timber Wagons

B928132 (Taken at Plumstead, S. E. London, 11/12/88)

S.E. London is not a place one would automatically associate with timber traffic but it is not that far away from the North Downs where many trees were blown down in the great hurricane of 1987. Thus the trunks were brought in by lorry to be dispatched by rail. Livery of B928132 is Flame Red sides, Rail Grey ends, black solebar and bogies and white lettering. (Ref: W14353/DL)

B. R. coped well with the unforeseen upsurge in timber traffic in the 1980s and suitable air-braked stock was quickly provided.

The BSW class shown above was a quick-fix solution which did not last very long. Known numbers are B927887, B928132 and B928193 and all had been converted to BDW previously.

The OTA class was derived from both OCA and VDA wagons, and as well as the various liveries carried, the modeller should note the considerable variation in the number and position of stanchions.

112324 (opposite upper) illustrates the first OCA-derived conversions, which had squared-off extensions to the OCA ends and eleven stanchions. Other known numbers were 112185/7 and 112225.

The next batch, although to the same design code OT001A, had higher, angled ends. These too had eleven stanchions, but had two additional stanchion positions. Known numbers were 112175/82, 112257/90, 112317/37/64/88 in BR livery, and 112182 and 112268 in light green/white SHOTTON PAPER livery.

OT001C wagons (as 112226, opposite centre) again had the higher ends but only nine stanchions, perhaps specified

by the original hirer, Thames Board Limited. These carried that firm's blue and white livery and known numbers were 112184/90, 112204/26, 112304/12/22.

OTAs converted from VDAs naturally retained the original van ends, but had only eight stanchions. Known numbers were 200721/40, 200814/22/39/61, 200933/48/65/6/82, 201029/61, 210193 and 210219 in BR livery, and 200822, 200948/68 and 201040 (opposite bottom) in two tone blue KRONOSPAN livery.

165 OTAs of all types were extant on 1/4/94, all being allocated to Transrail.

Right. *112324 (Taken at Cardiff, 6/6/92)*
Three distinct versions of the OTA can just be seen in this view. The main wagon, 112324, is a survivor of the original type with lower ends and is believed to have lasted into Privatisation. Livery is Flame Red with black solebar and white stanchions and lettering. (Ref: W17062/DL)

Centre. *112226 (Taken at Inverness, 15/6/92)*
Many OTAs received the colours of the firm to which the timber was being delivered. This example is in a now rusty blue livery for THAMES BOARD. The company name, originally in a white panel on the end has been painted out. Solebar is black. (Ref: W17114/DL)

Below. *201040 (Taken at Hoo Junction, 1/6/89)*
Most of the VDAs converted to OTAs were painted into KRONOSPAN livery and operated to Chirk, just over the Welsh border near Oswestry. The livery was light blue with the firm's name in dark blue/white on the end. Solebar was black. (Ref: W16242/DL)

Section 18. Air Braked Wagons for Nuclear Flask Traffic

550058 (Taken at Hither Green, 25/6/92)
Nuclear flask wagons are conveyed in dedicated trains all round the U.K. in basically pick-up/drop off freights calling at the nuclear power stations in rotation and ending up at the end of the week at Sellafield. Thus two or three flask wagons can be seen on a typical train, with barrier vehicles and one brake van. On 550058 the flask container casing is white, the chassis is buff and lettering is white on black. The bogies are black. (Ref: W17255/DL)

Only one type of FNA nuclear flask wagon is regularly seen in service today and this is illustrated above. Nos. 550015 to 550026 were built in B.R. workshops to design code FN 003A. 550027 to 550066 were built by Procor Ltd., Wakefield to design code FN 003F. The whole fleet passed to Transrail on 1/4/94, with the exception of No. 550019 which was deliberately destroyed in a high profile safety demonstration in July 1984.

To act as barrier wagons to this fleet, HEA hoppers were transferred and recoded FNA. Initially this was merely a transfer on paper and the vehicles were in unmodified condition (see 360323, opposite upper). When circumstances permitted, probably when the vehicle was due for a major overhaul, the bodywork was cut down (see 361164, opposite centre). This was probably to improve visibility of the flasks by the train guard.

At least one unusual vehicle was converted; 361798 (opposite lower) is one of the HEA class built with experimental springs. Note that in this photo, it has not been withdrawn, merely the buffers have been removed in the wagon repair shops at Carlisle Currock.

Numbers for the RNA fleet were 360046/69, 360211, 360323, 360492, 360592, 360630, 360716, 360808, 361001, 361105/12/64/84, 361253/74, 361394, 361484, 361522/61/81, 361627, 361738/9/74/98, 361867, 361900/68. 31 were extant on 1/4/94 and all went to Transrail.

360323 (Taken at Hither Green, 25/6/92)
This vehicle was a later addition to the RNA fleet and shows it with only the code changed. Livery is now a rusty Freight Brown body with black solebar and white lettering.
(Ref: W17254/DL)

361164 (Taken at Grove Park, 30/7/92)
The standard RNA retained enough of the original bodywork to illustrate its origins. There was enough space on the right hand end to apply the yellow/black sector symbol (almost obliterated by dirt here). Running in the refurbished sector livery, the body was dark grey, the chassis black and the lettering white. (Ref: W17296/DL)

361798 (Taken at Carlisle, 16/6/92)
When new, the HEA wagon type was used to try out various experimental suspension springs before B.R. adopted the Bruninghaus standard design seen above. This example has the Bruninghaus springs, but with vertical linkages, instead of the more usual angled linkages. Livery is as above. (Ref: W17180/DL)

Section 19. Warflats and Private Owner Container Flats

MODA95235 (Taken at Hoo Junction Yard, 8/89)
At the start of the review period, the M. o. D. were operating quite lengthy trains loaded with military vehicles. This was the end vehicle of one such train of Warflat wagons carrying Saxon armoured personnel carriers. Livery of the PFB is military green with black bogies and yellow lettering. (Ref: W16398/DL)

Having continued to use WWII vintage stock since 1945, the Ministry of Defence decided to update their railway wagon fleet during the mid 1970s. A totally new Warflat design (above) was produced by the BREL workshops at Shildon in 1976 and 1981. These vehicles were numbered MODA95233 to MODA95297 and were coded PFB, design code PF 004A.

Four-wheeled container vehicles in private ownership were uncommon and continental owned ones virtually unheard of. 23 70 442 4 005-7 (opposite upper) is one of a batch of four built in 1984 in France and on hire to S.T.S. Ltd. Number series was 23 70 442 4 001 – 2 to 23 70 442 4 005-7 and were coded KGA, design code KGE578.

Two designs of bogie container flat from this review period are illustrated opposite; both are basically similar in appearance. Owned by the wagon leasing firm Railease, RLS92548 is seen opposite centre in the service of Pedigree Petfoods at Melton Mowbray. This is one of a batch of four built in 1985 numbered RLS92547 to RLS92550 and coded PFA, design code PF 010A.

Tiphook owned TIPH93272 (opposite lower) seen in the service of Shanks and McEwan and carrying three sheeted

containers. This batch was built slightly later than the Railease ones, in 1987/88, and are seen with Gloucester GPS type bogies. The batch was numbered TIPH93242 to TIPH93281 and coded PFA, design code PF 010B.

Opposite Centre. *RLS92548 (Taken at Melton Mowbray, 21/2/89)*
These vehicles operated between Pedigree's factory at Melton Mowbray and Luton or Manchester. They ran with an additional, later built batch of 22 numbered RLS92610 to RLS92631. The flat is black with white lettering, container livery is brown. The dappled effect on the bodyside is caused by shadows of nearby trees - it is not a weathering effect! (Ref: W15208/DL)

Opposite lower. *TIPH93272 (Taken at Hoo Junction Yard, 10/4/91)*
The PFA seen here was on a short term contract carrying asbestos-contaminated soil from Chatham Dockyard to Stewartby landfill site. The containers were green, the flat had a blue solebar with black bogies and lettering in white. (Ref: W16557/DL)

Right. *23 70 442 4 005-7 (Taken at Hither Green, 28/7/88)*

These interesting vehicles have led a shadowy existence, spending much time in store. In 1985 they were observed at Middlesborough, Mossend and Welwyn but with no record of the traffic. In 1987 they carried sugar beet from Cantley/South Lynn to Glasgow(Deanside) or Gartcosh. There was again a fleeting mention of one at Boston in 1989, but all were in store by 1990. (Ref: W14063/DL)

Section 20. Private Owner 4 wheeled Opens

TRL5143 (Taken at Hoo Junction Yard, 9/4/92)
This vehicle was originally a ferry railtank, hence the end platform, and was rebuilt in 1985 for stone traffic (numbers TRL5143 to TRL5151, Design code PO 015A). Seen here in Foster Yeoman traffic from Isle of Grain, livery is light grey body, black solebar, black lettering and usual yellow/black YEOMAN logo.(Ref: W16793/DL).

TRL5314 (opposite upper) was part of a batch of vehicles built in 1988 using redundant railtank chassis. The whole batch was numbered TRL5312 to TRL5351 and coded POA, design code PO 016F. TRL5312 to TRL5340 were originally used by ARC between Pemaenmawr and Ashburys (Manchester). They were later seen operating for British Coal from Maryport to Padiham, as shown here.

TRL5370 (illustrated on page 6) is very similar, though with slightly different bodyside ribbing, and is in service with Foster Yeoman. This batch were numbered TRL5352 to TRL5385 and were also coded POA, design code PO 016J. Both batches were built by C. C. Crump Ltd., Connahs Quay. TRL 5143 (above) is an interesting variant, having been built on a redundant ferry railtank chassis.

RLS5229 (opposite centre) is part of the batch numbered RLS5214 to RLS5233 and was coded POA, design code PO 017A. They were built by Standard Wagon Ltd., Heywood in 1987 to capitalise on the then buoyant Speedlink network. RLS4560 to RLS4579 (not illustrated) are very similar but have the design code PO 018A. All operate for Allied Steel and Wire Ltd. of Cardiff, to and from South Wales with scrap.

PDUF4553 (opposite lower) operates for the same company but the owner of the wagon is Powell Duffryn. This batch was numbered PDUF4500 to PDUF4559 and the code was POA, design code is PO 016 X (note that the letter varies due to the origins of the ex-SUKO railtank chassis used).

There were many other POA designs operating throughout the review period, most of them being approximately the same length and having different heights depending on the load.

TRL5314 (Taken at Workington, 16/6/92)

This photo provides a good example of the sometimes rapid redeployment of wagons when a traffic ceases. TRL5314 originally worked stone traffic for ARC and still carried that livery but was seen here loaded with coal on a totally different working. Body is lime green with black solebar and white lettering. Grey ARC symbol and yellow/black Tiger symbol. (Ref: W17157/DL)

RLS5229 (Taken at Manchester, Ardwick, 24/10/88)

RLS5229 is a rebuild from earlier Railease owned TIP-AIR sodium carbonate powder tanks (see Vol. 2, pg. 41) and used the chassis from RLS12217. As tanks they had a fairly brief period in service, spending much of their time stored. Seen here in ASW use, the livery is black with yellow stripes and white lettering. The wire symbol is red, black and white. (Ref: W14170/DL)

PDUF4553 (Taken at Banbury, 1/4/92)

The ASW traffic was also conveyed in wagons owned by Powell Duffryn Ltd., which were of a slightly different body design, but still basically the same in concept. The livery of this batch was similar to above, but had no stripes. (Ref: W16725/DL

Section 21. Private Owner Bogie Open Wagons

33 70 679 0 032-0 (Taken at Hoo Junction Yard, 31/5/89)
Tiphook Rail Ltd. were a Kent-based firm who seem to have started up in the late 1980s with both lorries and railway wagons. This French-built bogie open aggregate wagon was used on the Channel Tunnel construction traffic. Livery is light grey with black bogies and white lettering on black panels. The logo is orange, blue and white. (Ref: W16175/DL)

Further examples of bogie box open wagons continued to appear during the review period, some new and some second hand, either refurbished or rebuilt.

33 70 679 0 032-0 (above) was part of a batch of new vehicles built in France in 1988/89. Number series was 33 70 679 0 000 -7 to 33 70 679 0 099 -1 and the code was JRA (JRE703). After the use mentioned in the caption ceased, some operated from Bardon Hill quarry and, much later, they began to appear in ballast trains on the old S.R. network.

The Foster Yeoman aggregate services continued to operate through this review period, using the second hand or rebuilt wagons acquired in the previous review period (refer to Vol. 3, section 26) supplemented by further rebuilds and some brand new vehicles. Most vehicles still had semi-permanent coupling arrangement and continued to operate in fixed rakes.

PR3169 (opposite upper) was one of a batch of JNAs built on 100T bogie railtank chassis in 1987 by Procor Ltd. PR3160 to PR3163 are the 'outer' wagons used in the fixed rakes with only one end retaining proper buffers, design code is JN 029F. PR3164 to PR3169 are 'inner' wagons with no buffers, design code JN 029E.

PR26554 (opposite centre) was a former British Steel vehicle and was one of a batch built in 1972/73 and coded JTA, design code JT 002F. Compare the livery with that of a vehicle from the same batch operating in the previous review period (Vol. 3, pg. 61.)

OK3328 (opposite lower) is an example of a new vehicle built in 1988 in Germany. This is an 'outer' wagon coded JYA, design code JY 012B. The whole batch was numbered OK3268 to OK3328 and, although they usually operated in rakes with vehicles of their own type, they could be occasionally seen with one of the other types.

Above. **PR3169 (Taken at Harlow Mill, 20/2/89)**

This wagon still carries the old PXA code but the livery should be compared with that in Vol. 3, pg. 61. The former railtank chassis was a bit long for this traffic and shorter, taller vehicles were preferred. Livery is light grey body, black solebar and bogies and white lettering on black panels. YEOMAN is the company's corporate blue and white and the PROCOR symbol red and white. (Ref: W15057/DL)

Centre. **PR26554 (Taken at Harlow Mill, 20/2/89)**

The former British Steel wagons were preferred for size, but the running gear was outmoded by the late 1980s. This one still carries the old PTA code. Livery is as above but looks a little weather worn here. (Ref: W15055/DL)

Right. **OK3328 (Taken at Hoo Junction, 12/1/89)**

Seen soon after arrival from the builders in Germany, this also carries the old PHA code. Livery is silver rather than light grey but is otherwise as above without the PROCOR symbol.
(Ref: W114824/DL)

Section 22. Private Owner 4-wheeled Hoppers

PR14692 (Taken at Allington Siding, 9/89)
Before the introduction of new bogie types (see Section 24), the ARC trains were formed of a variety of different PGA designs and painted in a number of liveries as well. This example had been in ARC service a long time and is in the house colours of Lime Green with black springs and white lettering on black panels but does not carry an ARC logo. The PROCOR symbol is red on white. (Ref: W16495/DL)

Rising stars of the 1970s, the four wheeled aggregate hoppers began their steady decline during this review period. PR14692 (above) was one of a batch built in 1975 by Standard Wagon Ltd., Heywood and numbered PR14688 to PR14704. Coded PGA under TOPS, design code PG 006B and is a development of the design illustrated in Vol. 2, pg. 54. All were in store by 1992.

TAMC14869 (opposite upper) was one of the design illustrated in Vol. 3, pg. 63. Built by Procor Ltd. in 1979/80 and seen here in 1989 sporting a livery variant. They were still operating between Whatley or Stud Farm quarries and Hayes, Middlesex in 1992.

SRW18505 (opposite centre) was one of a batch of rebuilds from former BSTE hoppers (see Vol. 3, pg. 63). Refurbished by Standard Wagon Ltd., Heywood, the batch

was numbered SRW18500 to SRW18529, TOPS code again PGA, design code PG 010B/C. It is seen here operating with TARMAC hoppers from Whatley quarry to Hothfield, all however were in store by 1992.

PR14340 (opposite lower) is in service with Foster Yeoman from the Isle of Grain. Part of a batch built in 1980 by Procor to design code PG 013E, PR14333 to PR14335, PR14337 to PR14341 and PR14382 to PR14388 were in Foster Yeoman use in 1992. PR14336 and PR14342 to PR14345 were with ARC at this time and ECC had PR14346 to PR14381.

TAMC14869 (Taken at Hothfield, 10/89)
*The white livery of the TARMAC hoppers (see Vol. 3, pg. 63) was becoming rather shabby by the late 1980s and this new livery was introduced. Body was dark green with black solebar and white lettering on black panels. The logo however was still black and the large revised lettering in white.
(Ref: W16547/DL)*

SRW18505 (Taken at Hothfield, 10/89)
*The hired SRW hoppers were rather colourful. The body is cream with black springs and black number. RAILEASE is blue and the RMC logo orange and black.
(Ref: W16539/DL)*

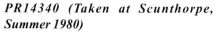
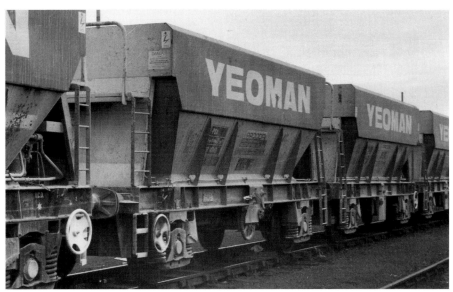

PR14340 (Taken at Scunthorpe, Summer 1980)
The PGA fleet operated by Foster Yeoman carried the same corporate colours as the bogie open wagons in the previous section and, unlike the four-wheeled POAs in section 20, carried the company name in full. Body then, is light grey with black solebar, corporate logo white on blue panel and other lettering, white on black panel. (Ref: W14401/DL)

Section 23. Private Owner Bogie Hoppers (1)

83 70 690 5 142-8 (Taken at Hoo Junction Yard, 5/5/89)
The European railway systems used hopper wagons of very different designs to those designed in the U.K. This French-built vehicle for instance, is rather unusual in appearance but very colourful. Bodywork is light grey with blue solebar, black bogies, black/ white lettering and striking blue, orange and white logo. (Ref: W16126/DL)

Tiphook Rail took in a number of overseas wagon designs in the late 1980s (see sections 21 and 35) of which the above is one example. This a French-built vehicle constructed in 1988 and is from the batch 83 70 690 5 100 -1 to 83 70 690 5 199 -3. The TOPS code was KPA and design code KPE702. Similar, but to design code KPE700, were 83 70 690 5 000 -2 to 83 70 690 5 049-5. The Tiphook fleet in general was built speculatively for 'spot hire' use and by 1992, most of these were operating exclusively on the European mainland.

HALL13710 (opposite upper) was from a batch built in 1984 by Standard Wagon Ltd. and operated from Newhaven to Crawley and Tolworth on sea-dredged aggregate traffic. The numbers were HALL13700 to HALL13712, the code being JGA and design code JG 009A. The Tolworth traffic actually ceased later in 1989 and the Crawley traffic went

by December 1992. The latter flow started up again but the vehicles had been transferred to Peak Forest by 1996.

BHQ17109 (opposite centre) is seen operating from Bardon Hill quarry to Angerstein Wharf, S.E. London. This batch, numbered BHQ17101 to BHQ17129, again coded JGA, design code JG 010A was built in 1986-88 by W.H. Davis Ltd., Langwith Junction.

Finally, RHR17320 (opposite lower) was also built by W. H. Davis Ltd., in 1987 in this case, and was part of the batch numbered RHR17301 to RHR17327, also coded JGA with design code JG 004C. These vehicles have spent time in store but do emerge on special traffics on occasions.

Above. **HALL13710 (Taken at Tolworth, 25/1/89)**
The brightly liveried HALL fleet carried sea-dredged aggregates from the South Coast to various inland distribution points. The hopper body is orange with white band, black solebar and bogies and black lettering. The diamond logo is black-lined orange. (Ref: W14842/DL)

Centre. **BHQ17109 (Taken at Hither Green, 2/4/92)**
The BARDON fleet conveys crushed granite from Bardon Hill quarry in Leicestershire to various points across the country, including Angerstein Wharf. The eyecatching livery consists of green bodywork with a yellow stripe and logo, black bogies and solebar with white lettering. (Ref: W16781/DL)

Right. **RHR17320 (Taken at Hoo Junction, 7/12/88)**
RH ROADSTONE is a subsidiary of Tarmac and one known destination for these vehicles was Marks Tey, Essex, which suggests that sand may have been conveyed at one time. Livery is pale green bodywork with white band, black solebar and bogies, white number. The RH ROADSTONE logo is black. (Ref: W14461/DL)

Section 24. Private Owner Bogie Hoppers (2)

ARC17908 (Taken at Hither Green, 2/4/92)
The prototype of the design shown here was built in 1988 by Standard Wagon Ltd. with buffers at each end. It was subsequently converted to an 'outer' to go with the 1990-built batch mentioned in the main text. ARC17908 shown here is an 'outer' vehicle and is painted in the house colour of lime green with logo in black. (Ref: W16752/DL)

The ARC fleet of hopper wagons operating at the start of the review period was rather elderly (see Section 22) and the company decided to invest in custom-built trains of bogie vehicles with semi-permanent rakes. These wagons were built by Standard Wagon Ltd. in 1990 and coded JHA, design code JH 017A. The number range was ARC17901 to ARC17931. To operate with them ARC19801 to ARC19891 (opposite upper) were built in 1990/91 as 'inner' vehicles without buffers. Again coded JHA, the design code is JH 016A.

A much smaller batch of these 'inner' hoppers, to a slightly different design was built in 1990 by Bombardier Prorail (formerly Procor Ltd.). This was possibly a contract to test out another company's product and was numbered ARC19892 to ARC19913. As before coded JHA, the design code for these was JH 018A. ARC19899 (opposite centre) is an example of this batch.

Something a bit different is represented by PR17815 (opposite lower). These had been constructed earlier in 1984 by Procor Ltd., Wakefield. The batch was numbered PR17801 to PR17837, of which PR17802/15/8/24/8/30 were 'outer' vehicles to design code PH 008C, the remainder being 'inners', as shown, to design code PH 008B. All were hired to Foster Yeoman and worked from Merehead quarry. They were however an unsuccessful design, the aluminium bodies not being sufficiently sturdy for the job. They were quickly consigned to the scrap heap, being totally deleted by 1992 and replaced with JHA hoppers similar in design to the ARC vehicles but built in Germany.

Right. ***ARC19813 (Taken at Hither Green, 2/4/92)***
The ends of these vehicles display a new shape in that the bodyside fairings extend beyond the hopper ends and partially shroud the sloped protective casings. This presumably is a development for aerodynamic reasons, reducing turbulence over the load and thus minimising dust dispersion. Livery is as opposite.
(Ref: W16743/DL)

Centre. ***ARC19899 (Taken at Hither Green, 2/4/92)***
The Procor version of the new ARC JHA hopper displays a similar design at the ends though with a shallower sloping protective cover. In most other respects, including the low track force bogies, it was very much the same as those above, as is the livery. (Ref: W16744/DL)

Below. ***PR17815 (Taken at Theale, 9/3/89)***
After a very short working life, new wagons to replace this unsuccessful design were delivered in 1989. The bodywork was in natural bright metal finish with YEOMAN logo in white on blue panel. Underframe and bogies were black with numbers in black. (Ref: W15480/DL)

Section 25. Private Owner Bulk Powder Wagons (1)

BCC10845 (Taken at Inverness, 15/6/92)
As mentioned in volume 3, T.O.P.S. prefix letters for the A.P.C.M. Co. fleet were changed from APCM to BCC in the early 1980s. BCC10845 (above) is an example of the company's own small batch of PCA 'Powderjet' vehicles still in use. Livery is grey with black solebar and lettering is either black, or white on black panel. (Ref: W17115/DL)

A.P.C.M. Co. Ltd. vehicles, with the Blue Circle Cement branding, have featured in each of the earlier volumes in this series. Extreme competition from overseas manufacturers, particularly in Greece, was having a drastic effect on the company and their large works at Northfleet closed during the review period. Despite this, their large fleet of 'chevron' wagons (see Vol. 2, pg. 34 and Vol. 3, pg. 71) and the small batch of BCC-owned French-built cement wagons to design code PC 017A were still operational in 1992. Scottish traffic was still being carried as seen above.

RLS10300 (opposite upper) is also a PCA for cement traffic. These vehicles were built in 1983 by Standard Wagon Ltd., Heywood and operated by Tunnel Cement Ltd. (See Vol. 3, pg. 73). This example is in the livery of Castle Cement Ltd., which operated from Clitheroe, Lancashire.

PR10007 (opposite centre) was originally used on soap powder traffic but is seen here conveying starch. From the

batch numbered PR10000 to PR10018 and built in 1976 by Procor Ltd, comparison of the various liveries carried by these vehicles can be made by reference to Vol. 2, pg. 73 and Vol. 3, pg. 72.

PR10107 (opposite lower) is rather similar, but with catwalk. The batch, numbered PR10100 to PR10124, design code PC 015C, was also built by Procor, but a bit later in 1980/81. They were again coded PCA and seen in use here carrying sodium carbonate.

RLS10300 (Taken at Warrington Arpley, 23/10/88)
An interesting study over the four volumes of this series show each wagon builder used subtly different shapes of tank barrel for cement wagon designs. Livery on this example is light grey with black solebar, black lettering and red CASTLE CEMENT lettering and logo. (Ref: W14156/DL)

PR10007 (Taken at Manchester, Ardwick, 24/10/88)
As outlined in the main text, this particular batch of PCAs had seen quite a few liveries during their career. Here, this very colourful livery has a white tank, black solebar with white numbers on black panels. The company lettering is black with leaf logo in bright green. The CAIB symbol is red on white.(Ref: W14175/DL)

PR10107 (Taken at Larbert, 27/10/88)
The Larbert soda ash traffic has seen a plethora of wagon designs and liveries. This one has tank body and solebar in a cream shade with black springs and white number on black panels. Company lettering and logo is in black and PROCOR is red on white. (Ref: W14273/DL)

Section 26. Private Owner Bulk Powder Wagons (2)

PR11306 (Taken at Manchester, Ardwick, 24/10/88)
The PBA shown here, soon to be coded JBA, was another type to be seen in a number of liveries. First illustrated in Vol. 3, pg. 67, following their transfer from tripolyphosphate traffic, they carried the CPC livery for a time (not illustrated). It is seen here carrying the white 'Cerestar' livery as detailed on the previous page. (Ref: W14171/DL)

In the days of the traditional B.R. standard wagon, these vehicles would have been termed 'Covhops', (see Vol. 3, page 64-69 and earlier volumes) but such terms fell into disuse with the advent of T.O.P.S.

The type illustrated by PR11306 (above) was quite an early design of bogie powder wagon having been built by Charles Roberts Ltd. in 1972. Some were withdrawn after an accident but the survivors, numbered PR11300/4 – 6/8/ 9/11/2, were in use on the Ardwick starch traffic in 1992. Now coded JBA, design code was JB 002A.

33 70 929 2 214 -1 (opposite upper) is listed as a bogie tank wagon but the general appearance of it suggests a bulk powder wagon. This example, and one other (205-9), were recorded in starch traffic in 1992, although another record shows them not working in the U.K. at that time. The batch was built in France in 1987/88 and was numbered 33 70 929 2 200 - 0 to 33 70 929 214 -1.

The POLYBULK hoppers in china clay traffic had first appeared in 1974/75 (see Vol. 2, pg. 40) and were still operating on European traffic in 1992. 33 70 938 2 050-0 (opposite centre) is part of a batch coded JIB, design code JIE431, and numbered 33 70 938 2 000 -5 to 33 70 938 2 058 -6. This one is seen in Traffic Services Ltd. livery.

The Grainflow POLYBULK hoppers were featured in Vol. 3, pg. 69 and 33 70 938 5 009 -3 (opposite lower) shows a subtle livery variation. These vehicles, also coded JIB, design code JIE518, were part of a further batch built in 1983 and numbered 33 70 938 5 000-2 to 33 70 938 5 029-9.

Few new 'Covhop' designs seem to have been developed after those shown here, although the china clay POLYBULK hoppers, for instance, remained in service for many years, only being recently replaced at the time of writing. Such lack of further development would suggest a connection with the general trend towards container traffic.

Opposite lower. ***33 70 938 5 009-3 (Taken at Avonmouth Docks, 11/3/89)***
Avonmouth docks has been a regular haunt of grain wagons from as far back as G.W.R. days and it is good to record such traffic still extant in Polybulks during the review period. (Ref: W15697/DL)

33 70 929 2 214-1 (Taken at Aberdeen, 15/6/92)
This design resembles a bogie version of the French-built cement wagon on page 58, which is why I suggest it is not a railtank despite the TIA code. Livery is similar to that as opposite but this has the addition of the TIPHOOK logo in white and blue. (Ref: W17123/DL)

Centre. ***33 70 938 2 050-0 (Taken at Coalville, 22/2/89)***
Well weathered in china clay dust, this wagon was at Marcroft Wagon Ltd., for overhaul. Livery is green and grey with black solebar and bogies. Numbers and lettering are in white with TRAFFIC SERVICES Ltd. in yellow. The TSL logo is pink, black and white.
(Ref: W15238/DL)

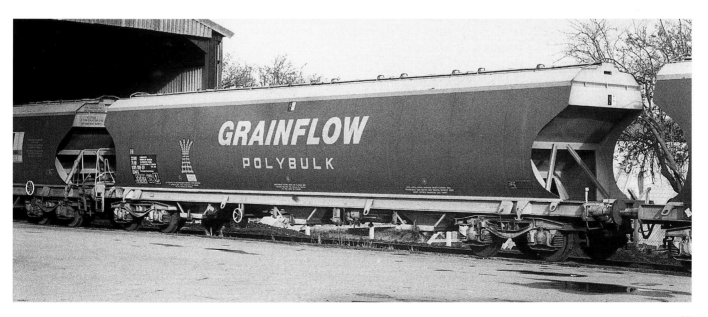

Section 27. Private Owner Bulk Powder Wagons (3)

BSGL8163 (Taken at Mossend, 26/10/88)
Although Ravenscraig had ceased steel production the year before, these wagons are still listed in a 1992 record. Livery is weathered grey with black solebar and white lettering. (Ref: W14232/DL)

In this section, we examine some bulk powder wagons of bottom discharge hopper design, a type more usually associated with granular commodities.

BSGL8163 (above) was built in 1975 by BREL Ashford Works and was coded PBA, design code PB008A/B. These vehicles operated between Hardendale Quarry, Shap and Ravenscraig Steelworks with crushed limestone and outlived the 1979 built PGA type which was also used on this traffic (see Vol. 3., pg. 65). The batch was numbered BSGL8150 to BSGL8199 and they were notable by having a slightly longer wheelbase than other contemporary designs.

CPL14174 (opposite upper), is an example of another long wheelbase design built in 1975 by Procor Ltd., Wakefield, and coded PAA. It had originally been in service with I.C.I. Agricultural, operating between Duxford and Haverton Hill, but by 1992, had passed onto Cleveland Potash workings on the Boulby mine branch. The design code was PA009B and the batch was now numbered CPL14156 to CPL14175.

Cleveland Potash operated mainly bogie vehicles, some originally built in 1974 (see Vol. 3, pg. 67). CPL17454 (opposite centre) is from a batch of new vehicles built specifically for this traffic in 1991 by W. H. Davis Ltd. The batch was coded JGA, design code JG012A, and was numbered CPL17450 to CPL17456.

33 88 928 2 009-7 (opposite lower) is another example of the POLYBULK hopper first examined in Vol. 3., pg. 69 and represents a later livery variant. These types were for more general use, in traffic other than china clay or grain. Coded IRB, design code IRE442, and also built in 1974, the batch was numbered 33 88 928 2 000-6 to 33 88 928 2 009-7.

Opposite Centre. **CPL17454 (Taken at Middlesborough, 26/6/92)**
The new bogie hoppers for Cleveland Potash were to contemporary standards and dropped the overall hinged roof found on the type illustrated in Vol. 3, pg. 67. Livery is dark green with black solebar and bogies. Lettering is white. (Ref: W17266/DL)

Opposite lower. **33 88 928 2 009-7 (Taken at Hoo Junction Yard, 20/6/89)**
This wagon was Belgian-registered and was owned by CAIB in 1992, and judging by its location was operating on continental traffic. This livery is light grey with black bogies and white lettering on black panels. The CITA logo is blue on white. (Ref: W16272/DL)

CPL14174 (Taken at Middlesborough, 26/6/92)
These vehicles look very much like bulk grain wagons but most of the build appear to have been used on the bulk urea traffic previously carried in B.R. Covhop wagons (see Vol. 3, pg. 23). By the time this photo was taken, all the batch had been transferred to CPL traffic. The livery was as below.
(Ref: W17262/DL)

Section 28. Private Owner Railtanks (China clay)

TRL70709 (Taken at Aberdeen, 15/6/92)
Originally built for caustic soda liquor and later used on china clay slurry traffic, this vehicle is in the E.C.C. blue livery with black solebar and white number on black panel. The ECC symbol and lettering is white and the TIGER logo is yellow and black. (Ref: W17120/DL)

China clay in a liquid suspension form known as 'slurry' was conveyed in a number of diverse tank designs during the review period. Apart from some early railtanks in Bowaters' traffic, very few four wheeled designs were used, although one of this type is represented by TRL70709 (above). Built in 1977 by Standard Wagon, it was originally part of a batch of caustic soda liquor tanks (see Vol. 3, pg. 79). By 1990 all the batch, numbered TRL70700 to TRL70727 and coded TUA, were operating as china clay slurry tanks, although not all with E.C.C. International.

TRL78800 (opposite centre) is one of the French built batch numbered TRL78800 to TRL78804, coded TCA, with design code TC 009B, and previously recorded in this traffic in Vol. 3, pg. 83 but now fully repainted in E.C.C. International livery.

TRL86903 (opposite top) is rather an unusual design, it used the tanks of former four wheeled railtanks mounted on redundant bogie oil tank chassis. These vehicles were numbered TRL86895 to TRL86906 and were coded TDA, design code TD 011A.

Finally, 33 70 789 5 161-9 (opposite lower) is a German

built bogie design dating from 1985/86 coded TIB (design code TIE554). The whole batch was numbered between 33 70 789 5 151 - 5 to 3 70 789 5 165 - 9, but not all were used by E.C.C. International. The rest were hired to I.C.I. Organics on services from Haverton Hill on Tees-side to European destinations.

Opposite Centre. *TRL78800 (Taken at Hoo Junction, 11/2/89)*
This distinctive design was built in France in 1975, and as far as I have been able to ascertain, there were no others like it. Certainly in slurry traffic since modification from sulphuric acid use in 1981 (see Vol. 3, pg. 83), it was painted in the E.C.C. blue livery c. 1987. (Ref: W14971/DL)

Opposite Lower. *33 70 7895 161 - 9 (Taken at Hoo Junction, 17/12/88)*
Unlike the other vehicles in the E.C.C. china clay slurry traffic, these tanks retained the livery of the German owner - VTG. Livery is dark grey with black solebar and bogies and white lettering. VTG lettering is white and the logo is orange. All tanks on this page were photographed whilst on Bowaters' traffic operating between Sittingbourne and Cornwall. (Ref: W14359/DL)

Right. ***TRL86903 (Taken at Hoo Junction, 17/12/88)***
The thinking behind this particular rebuild may appear a bit obscure, although it may have been due to availability of component parts at the time. It does at least make for a very different design that could have come from a modeller's scrap box! Built in 1987 by C. C. Crumps, livery and markings are as below. (Ref: W14357/DL)

Section 29. Private Owner 4-wheeled Railtanks (1)

ESSO56135 (Taken at Harlow Town, 20/2/89)
The traditional 45tonne G.L.W. four wheeled railtank of the Esso fleet could still be seen operating in considerable numbers during the review period. They were often rather grubby and oil stained - though the dark area on the end of this vehicle is a shadow from an overhead gantry! Livery on this vehicle is still the standard Class A grey tank with red solebar, black springs and black lettering and markings. (Ref: W15088/DL)

During this review period, stability in the railtank fleet began to return following earlier rationalisations in the late 1970s and early 1980s. These had decimated the once numerous 45 tonne G.L.W. four-wheelers and some of the newer 51 tonners as well as a small selection of bogie tankers. In this section we focus on the time-honoured old favourites - the 45 tonners associated with the major oil companies; Esso, BP Oil, and Shell (UK).

Esso Ltd. still operated a fairly large quantity of these tanks dating from the early 1960s, as seen above; ESSO56135 is from the batch numbered ESSO56000 to ESSO56199 built in 1965 by R. Y. Pickering Ltd., Motherwell and coded TTA, design code TT 043R.

B.P. Oils Ltd. (BPO) also had some R. Y. Pickering Ltd. tanks, this time built in 1967. BPO67067 (opposite upper) was part of a batch BPO67060 to BPO67099, coded TTA, design code TT 026X. This company was refurbishing its fleet of 45 tonne tanks and at a time around Sectorisation, c. 1987, certain rules governing railtank livery were relaxed, allowing some Class A vehicles to appear in company house colours. BPO37291 (opposite centre) illustrates this, it was originally BPO66192 and was part of the batch BPO37260 to BPO37297.

Shell (U.K.) Ltd. (SUKO) fleet was still operational and SUKO65610 (opposite lower) has been partially repainted into its new house livery, this is a 1966-built tank and is part of the batch SUKO65600 to SUKO65659 allocated to diesel oil traffic.

BPO67067 *(Taken at Grain, 5/5/89)*
The B.P. Isle of Grain oil refinery closed down during the review period and the tanks seen at this location would soon be transferred elsewhere. This vehicle is quite oil stained and is also still in Class A tank livery, as opposite. (Ref: W16130/DL)

BPO37291 *(Taken at Inverness, 15/6/92)*
With rules on livery previously relaxed, new tanker colours could be seen on the railscene. Here the tank barrel is in B.P. Emerald Green, with yellow solebar and black springs. The traditional BP outline logo is yellow and Oil Sector logo yellow/blue. (Ref: W17117/DL)

SUKO65610 *(Taken at Hoo Junction, 8/89)*
For its 'new' livery, Shell (U.K.) Ltd. retained black overall with a 'designer' red and yellow stripe. This example sports only half the new livery, as it lacks red and yellow stripes, but bears the red/yellow SHELL logo. Other lettering is white. (Ref: W16445/DL)

Section 30. Private Owner 4-Wheeled Railtanks (2)

PR58618 (Taken at Peterborough, 30/5/92)
Class B railtanks for non petroleum based products had always been more colourful and this one is no exception, despite being rather dirty. The tank is split vertically into yellow/blue/yellow sections with the ends being yellow. Solebar is black, the numbers, white on black panels and the CAIB symbol red and white. (Ref: W16979/DL)

The smaller owners of tank wagons were also well represented in the four-wheeled railtank category, sometimes carrying commodities far different to what they were initially built for.

PR58618 (above) was originally a caustic soda liquor tank built by Standard Wagon Ltd., c. 1970, but has been converted c. 1984, to carry molasses with the fitting of heating coils (on the opposite end). This converted fleet was numbered PR58602 – 4/6/7/10/3 – 22/4/6/32/5/9 – 42/4/6/7/50/1/3 – 5/8/60 and was coded TTA, design code TT 053K.

PR58105 (opposite upper) was built in 1968 by Standard Wagon Ltd., Heywood as a Class A petrol tank, however, it is not in that traffic here. Ciba-Geigy Ltd. was one of the hirers of the batch numbered PR58101 to PR58135, which was coded TTB, design code TT 024A/B.

Still operating in its original traffic is BPO59665 (opposite centre), an L.P.G. tank. It was formerly ALG49316 built in 1966 with vacuum brakes. As with all such vehicles, there were various modifications and upgrades and the batch became BPO59660 to BPO59683, coded TTA and design code TT 001T.

The CO_2 tanks were still in full operation. STS53215 (opposite lower) is part of a 1966-built batch numbered STS53200 to STS53218. Comparison with STS53209 in Vol. 3, pg. 78 shows slight livery variations and new T.O.P.S. code; all were in the process of being recoded TTA from TTB when the vacuum through-pipes were removed. The design code was TT 018E.

PR58105 (Taken at Hexham, 28/10/88)
The commodity carried by this tank at this time is believed to be synthetic resin from the Ciba Giegy plant at Duxford (see section 30). Livery is pale blue for the tank, black solebar and white lettering. The old PROCOR logo is the usual red, black and white.
(Ref: W14284/DL)

BPO59665 (Taken at Inverness, 15/6/92)
One upgrade to almost all L.P.G. tanks was the fitting of buffer override protection plates, this vehicle has also been resprung with the Bruninghaus type. Livery for these tanks was still mandatory and it retains the white tank with orange band, black solebar, white number on black panel, red end number and other black markings.
(Ref: W17116/DL)

STS53215 (Taken at Bow Goods, 19/2/89)
The CO_2 tanks were also bound by the same regulations as the L.P.G. tanks and this vehicle also retains the same basic livery. The number is black and the STS logo is red and white.
(Ref: W14989/DL)

Section 31. Private Owner Bogie Railtanks

TRL86874 (Taken at Hexham, 28/10/88)
Judging by the very clean condition of this vehicle, it may have recently been refurbished and lagged for the Ciba-Geigy synthetic resin traffic. Livery is light grey tank, black solebar and bogies, black lettering on white panel and yellow and black TIGER symbol. (Ref: W14280/DL)

Bogie railtanks could still be seen in regular use in the review period, but they did not feature much in the larger oil company fleets.

TRL86874 (above) was built as a petrol tank but certainly appears here to have been modified for a different commodity (see caption). The full batch was numbered TRL86848 to TRL86888 with vehicles TRL86870/2/4/6/86/7 being ones that appear to have been used for the Ciba-Geigy traffic. These are coded TEA, design code TE 006E.

BRT84098 (opposite upper) was the only tank actually listed by T.O.P.S. as being for the resin traffic and was part of a batch built in 1968. Numbers for this batch are BRT84095 to BRT84098, the code is TEA and the design code, TE 007C.

BRT84196 (opposite centre) is a slightly more modern tank built in 1971 with Schlieren bogies. It appears to be on hire to Gulf Oils operating from Milford Haven refinery and is part of a batch numbered BRT84193 to BRT84200. The code is TEA, design code TE 021P.

More modern still is PR85312 (opposite lower), built in 1981. This batch is on hire to Murco and is numbered PR85300 to PR85317, coded TEA, design code TE 030.

Opposite Centre. ***BRT84196 (Taken at West Drayton, 2/6/92)***
Judging by the location of this vehicle and the logo on the tank, this vehicle may be carrying a load of aviation spirit. Tank is light grey with red logo, solebar red and bogies black. The number is white on black. (Ref: W17035/DL)

Opposite lower. ***PR85312 (Taken at Cardiff, 6/6/92)***
The modern bogie railtanks were constructed with a single ladder at each end, as seen here and with BRT84196. Livery is blue upper tank, white band, red lower tank, black solebar and white lettering on black panels. MURCO logo is white and CAIB is red and white. (Ref: W17057/DL)

Right. ***BRT84098 (Taken at Hexham, 28/10/88)***
This tank is an elderly lagged Class B vehicle and formed part of a mixed train of tanks conveying synthetic resin from Duxford. Livery is dirty black with black/red/white BRT logo. (Ref: W14281/DL)

Section 32. Ferry Railtanks

33 80 799 8 002-9 (Taken at Hoo Junction, 7/89).
Hoo Junction continued to play host to ferry railtanks during the review period and such traffic increased from 1987 following the closure of the Harwich route. This German-owned bogie railtank built in 1980 was probably one of the ones that had been re-routed as Harwich had usually dealt with consignments from northern parts of Europe and the Baltic. Livery is dark grey with black solebar and bogies, the lettering is white and the DEGUSSA name and logo is black.

The review period saw significant changes to traffic patterns of railtanks carrying dangerous and hazardous chemicals following the closure of the Harwich train ferry on 31st January 1987. All such traffic had then to be routed via Dover until it stopped altogether in late 1995.

33 80 799 8 002-9 (above) was part of a small batch numbered 33 80 799 8 000-3 to 33 80 799 8 004-5. TOPS code was ICB and design code ICE519. With other similar tanks of design code ICE548, they carried metallic sodium from Germany to Dee Marsh during the review period.

23 70 739 0 406-0 (opposite upper) was one of two vehicles built in 1964 by Charles Roberts, the other being 23 70 739 0 399-7. The design code for these was TIE704 and they were part of six similar TIAs carrying aqueous amines from ICI Haverton Hill to mainland Europe.

23 70 727 7 362-3 (opposite centre) was part of a batch of tanks designed to carry liquid gas and was also built by Charles Roberts in 1962. The batch was numbered 23 70 727 7 353-4 to 23 70 727 7 372-4, TOPS code TIX and design code TIE313. In their early years they were used in

various LPG traffics but by the review period, any not stored out of use were also carrying chemicals from ICI Haverton Hill to Europe, this time anhydrous amines.

German designed four-wheeled railtanks generally tended to be longer than contemporary British designs and 23 80 739 1 034-7 (opposite lower) illustrates this point well. The batch was numbered 223 80 739 1 026-1 to 23 80 739 1 034-7. The TOPS code was IBB and the design code IBE372. During the review period, they carried the industrial chemical, glycol, a coolant additive, from Germany to Middlesborough.

23 80 739 1 034-7 (Taken at Middlesborough, 13/6/92)
Glycol traffic from Germany seems to have been running for many years as examples were recorded in the 1950s. This example appears to date from the late 1960s, livery is dark grey for the tank, black solebar and white lettering. The VTG letters and logo are white. (Ref: W17091/DL)

23 70 739 0 406-0 (Taken at Hoo Junction, 8/89)
The brake platform tacked onto a more or less standard design makes for an interesting variation for modelling purposes, especially as the running gear appears to still be in its as-built condition. Livery is class A, with the mandatory grey tank, red solebar and black springs. ICI and AQUEOUS AMINES are black, TIGER logo black and yellow, and other lettering in white. (Ref: W16397A/DL)

23 70 727 7 362-3 (Taken at Hither Green, 28/7/88)
Although long out of such traffic, this vehicle has been designed to carry liquid gases from the UK to Europe and was fitted with a curved sunshield over the tank top. This item was not fitted to similar UK based stock. The mandatory liquid gas livery of white tank with orange band, black solebar and white or black lettering was applied. (Ref: W14082/DL)

Section 33. 4-wheeled Ferry Vans

21 83 238 2 241-9 (Taken at Hither Green, 28/7/88)
Very few examples of the traditional plank bodied long wheelbase ferry vans of the 1960s were to be seen at the start of the review period and most of those remaining soon disappeared. This Italian van is dark brown with a grey roof, black solebar and white lettering and markings. (Ref: W14064/DL)

Traditional designs of four-wheeled ferry vans were not seen in large numbers during the review period and the term eventually became synonymous with the modern all-metal vehicles seen on the opposite page.

Some examples still around include 21 83 238 2 241-9 (above) which was part of a batch of Italian vans coded ILB, design code ILE651, and described as a 'large van'. The number series was 21 83 238 2 000-6 to 21 83 238 2 299-5.

21 87 238 0 783-8 (opposite upper) is a French-owned van of plywood construction, once very common and also described as a 'large van'. Comparison with a similar vehicle in Vol. 2, pg. 53 shows that, other than renumbering, they altered very little during the intervening years. This batch was coded ILX, design code ILE304, and numbers during this period were 21 87 238 0 500-6 to 21 87 238 0 999-0.

24 71 239 6 026-9 (opposite centre) is a Spanish-owned van and is part of a batch built in 1984. It is to a contemporary design featuring all metal construction with sliding wall sides and described as a 'medium van', coded ITX, design code ITE575. The numbers for this batch were 24 71 239 6 000-4 to 24 71 239 6 199-2.

Finally, still relatively new on the scene during the review period were the semi-permanently coupled German-owned 45T twin set vans coded IZA of which the prototype pair is shown opposite lower. Very similar in design to the B.R. VGA type (see page 23), the production batch appeared in natural metal finish with the yellow and blue CARGOWAGGON logo split into two across both vehicles. They were used in the U.K. on Guinness, Spillers and Rover Group workings.

Opposite Centre. ***24 71 239 6 026-9 (Taken at Hoo Junction, 19/6/89)***
These all-metal sliding wall vans are also rather similar to the B.R. VGA van, except for the vertically sliding vents which are seen in the open position here. Roof and solebar are black, sides are again natural metal with TRANSFESA logo in blue and red. (Ref: W16243/DL)

Opposite Lower. ***23 80 239 8 500-1=23 80 239 8 501-9 (Taken at Mossend, 26/10/88)***
This pair is the prototype of the German 45T twin set vans. The livery was also the natural metal finish, but the yellow and blue CARGOWAGGON marking was applied whole on each vehicle in this unique pair, as seen here. Solebars are also blue and springs are black. (Ref: W14230/DL)

Right. ***21 87 238 0 783-8 (Taken at Hoo Junction, 7/89)***
As mentioned in Volume 2, the French-owned ferry vans were painted in a lighter shade of brown, similar to the old B.R. Bauxite colour. The roof is grey, the solebar black, and lettering is in white.
(Ref: W16324/DL)

Section 34. Bogie Ferry Vans (1)

33 80 279 6 097-4 (Taken at Avonmouth Docks, 11/3/89)
These vehicles were a common sight in the U.K. for a number of years, indeed dating back to the late 1970s. Livery is black roof, with silver sides and ends, black underframe and bogies. Lettering is white, with the arrow, logo and VTG lettering in black. The word FERRYWAGON is white. (Ref: W15698/DL)

Bogie ferry vans were first examined in Volume 3 (pg. 85) and the types, though not always of new designs, began to appear in increasing quantities during this review period.

33 80 279 6 097-4 (above) was built in 1977 and was part of a batch numbered 33 80 279 6 000-8 to 33 80 279 6 139-4. These were coded IWB (design code IWE471) and were seen on various duties, both on ferry services to and from Europe and within the U.K. itself.

33 80 279 7 607-6 (opposite upper) is also coded IWB, design code IWE512, and was built in 1979/80. These were also found on various duties including hired ones on Rover Group traffic. The batch was numbered 33 80 279 7 580-6 to 33 80 279 7 699-4.

33 80 279 7 716-8 (opposite centre) is similar again, but dates from 1983 and, lacking vacuum through pipes, is coded IWA, with design code IWE551. Used on similar traffic to that above, the batch was numbered 33 80 279 7 700-0 to 33 80 279 7 734-9.

Something different is 83 80 474 1 089-2 (opposite lower). This is described as a 'holdall van' and is coded IWA, design code IWE690. They were hired to Kemira and Norsk Hydro and each type could be seen working with other bogie vans in fertiliser traffic (see page 79, lower picture). Numbers were 83 80 474 1 001-7 to 83 80 474 1 160-1.

Opposite. *33 80 279 7 716-8 (Taken at Hoo Junction, 7/89)*
This provides a good detail shot of the distinctive end of this class of vehicle. The lack of vacuum pipe makes this an IWA. The livery is a later version also with natural metal bodywork, black solebar and bogies. The lettering is white on black and the CARGOWAGGON lettering is blue on a yellow panel. (Ref: W16323/DL)

33 80 279 7 607-6 *(Taken at Hoo Junction, 7/89)*
This type of ferry van is very much like a bogie version of the B.R. VGA van. This one is in an early style livery with natural metal sides, black solebar and bogies with white lettering on black panels. The central section has blue lettering on a long white panel. (Ref: W16321/DL)

83 80 474 1 089-2 *(Taken at Andover, 9/3/89)*
The so-called 'holdall vans' were an interesting development built in 1987. The hand wheels on the end are used for opening and moving the sliding sidewalls. The livery is natural metal with blue panels for the CARGOWAGGON lettering which is yellow. Black solebar and bogies and white lettering on black panels complete the colour scheme. (Ref: W15496/DL)

Section 35. Bogie Ferry Vans (2)

33 70 474 6 173-2 (Taken at Warrington Arpley Yard, 23/10/88)
Although this vehicle appears to be similar to the others in this section, it is rather deceptive in that it is not for general cargo. It is a strip coil wagon rather like the JGA class (see page 5). The hood is light grey, the vehicle ends blue, solebar and bogies are black and lettering is white. The TIPHOOK logo and lettering are blue, orange and white. (Ref: W14135/DL)

Bogie ferry vans with nylon hoods enjoyed a brief term of popularity during the review period but they did not command prolonged use in the U.K. The vehicles are all quite similar in appearance with the most noticeable difference being the liveries carried on the curtain sides. In the main they were general purpose vehicles but some operated on specialised traffic.

For instance, 33 70 474 6 173-2 (above) is, in fact, a strip coil wagon rather than a general purpose van. Built in France in 1987/88, the batch was numbered 33 70 474 6 100-5 to 33 70 474 6 179-9 and they operated throughout the U.K. on various steel carrying duties. They were coded KHA, design code KHE684.

33 87 474 6 045-4 (opposite upper) was built a little earlier, in 1983 in fact, and was coded IUA. The design code was IUE545. Used on general traffic to and from Europe, this batch was numbered 33 87 474 6 020-6 to 33 87 474 6 049-5.

83 87 473 9 023-9 (opposite centre) was also built in 1983 but differs by being fitted with vacuum through pipes for operating within the Spanish Transfesa network, it was thus coded IUB (design code IUE545). The number series

was 83 87 473 9 020-5 to 83 87 473 9 024-7 and were also used on general duties.

33 87 474 6 018-0 (opposite lower) is one of a batch used on fertiliser traffic from the Norsk Hydro plant at Immingham. Built in 1986, this batch is coded IUA, design code IUE672, and is numbered 33 87 474 6 012-3 to 33 87 474 6 019-8.

Opposite Centre. *83 87 473 9 023-8 (Taken at Hoo Junction, 5/89)* *This example is also in blue with the TRANSFESA fleetname in red. Solebar and bogies are again black with other lettering in white. The retention of the vacuum through pipe may have been required for operations in Spain. (Ref: W16147/DL)*

Opposite Lower. *33 87 474 6 018-0 (Taken at Hoo Junction, 5/89)* *The livery applied to this vehicle included a rather bold design representing the company logo. The hood and vehicle ends were blue with black solebar and bogies and white lettering. The company logo was white. (Ref: W16203/DL)*

Right. ***33 87 474 6 045-4 (Taken at Hoo Junction, 5/89)***
The majority of the curtain sided vans were French owned and, although this one is listed as being owned by Cargowaggon, it carries the fleetname TRANSFERRY in yellow. Hood and ends are again blue, solebar and bogies are black and other lettering is white. (Ref: W16144/DL)

Section 36. Private Owner Car-carrying Wagons

MAT90384/5/6/7 (Taken at Hoo Junction, 7/89)
The CARTIC-4 double-deck car-carrying sets had been around since the 1960s and remained in use throughout the review period. As a consequence of theft and vandalism, protective screening was fitted from the late 1970s onwards. The bodywork is blue, bogies are black and all lettering white. (Ref: W16367/DL)

Car traffic continued to be carried throughout the review period, this included both U.K. built vehicles shipped to distribution centres and for export, and imported cars shipped from various ports. It was, however, rather a seasonal traffic in that more would be seen operating through the summer months on the run up to the August registration date.

MAT90384-7 (above) represents the elderly, but still very useful CARTIC-4 bogie articulated sets that had been in continuous use since the mid-1960s, although this particular batch, numbered from MAT90160/1/2/3 to MAT90396/7/8/9 was built in 1970/71 by BREL Ashford Works. The sets by now were coded PJA, with various design codes. As usual with articulated, permanently coupled sets only the outer ends of the outer vehicles are fitted with buffers and drawgear. Cartic-4 fleets were operated by several owners including the major vehicle distributors, MAT Transauto, Silcock & Colling and Toleman.

Similar in shape to the Cartic-4s, but built as individual bogie wagons c. 1979-81, are the Procor 80s (not illustrated). These operated on similar services as the Cartic-4s

throughout the review period.

The remainder of the views in this section are based on the French-built 3-axle articulated AUTIC design built c.1981 and show some of the various screens fitted to increase protection for the load. The batch as a whole was coded PQA and the sets were numbered RLS92000+RLS92001 to RLS92110+RLS92111. They were owned by the wagon leasing firm Railease and hired to various operators.

RLS92013=RLS92012 (opposite upper) represents the basic vehicle without screens and is in service with Renault.

RLS92055=RLS92054 (opposite centre) shows a set with mesh screens fitted along the sides. MAT Transauto is the operator here.

RLS92079=RLS92078 (opposite lower) is of a vehicle operating for Carter from Queenborough, Kent. This one has been fitted opaque plastic side screens and a corrugated roof which is pneumatically raised for loading. Similar screens and roof were fitted to some of the Cartic-4 sets, the Silcock fleet having been recorded so fitted.

RLS92013=RLS92012 (Taken at Warrington Arpley, 23/10/88)
This illustration of the PQA Autic shows the basic design without any screening. It was recorded here in the yellow livery of Renault, the brand name located on a white panel. Running gear is black and numbering is black on white panel.
(Ref: W14136/DL)

RLS92055=RLS92054 (Taken at Hoo Junction, 22/6/89)
This set is fitted with metal mesh side screens of similar construction to those opposite. Livery is the blue house colours of the operator MAT Transauto.
(Ref: W16306/DL)

RLS92079=RLS92078 (Taken at Hoo Junction, 4/89)
The full side screens and roof offered the best protection and helped to obscure the load from prying eyes. The roof is dark grey, bodywork is in the orange Silcock house colour, and the side panels are buff coloured plastic. Lettering is white on black panels.
(Ref: W16117/DL)

Section 37. Private Owner Open Wagons (PLASMOR)

PLAS5427 (Taken at Biggleswade, 20/2/89)
This Plasmor POA is seen unloaded and ready for its return journey with the hinged sides folded flat onto the floor. The livery was colourful with orange ends, green sides, black solebar and white lettering on black panels. (Ref: W15100/DL)

A new source of regular rail traffic which began just prior to the review period was the transhipment of loads of 'breeze' blocks from private sidings at Heck, on the East Coast Main Line near Doncaster. The company, Plasmor Ltd, makes use of pulverised fuel ash from the nearby Aire Valley coal fired power stations in the manufacture of these blocks. The regular supply of this material no doubt helped to secure a long term commitment to rail. Destinations include Biggleswade, Bow and Willesden.

The vehicles used included a fleet actually owned by Plasmor. These were rebuilt from former B.R. VCA vans by W. H. Davis Ltd., in 1988/89 (see above and opposite upper). They were given special hinged sides to assist with loading/unloading and were coded PNA, design code PN019A. The number range was PLAS5269 to PLAS5293 and PLAS5417 to PLAS5446.

Working with these vehicles were converted OBAs which formed the original hired fleet of wagons for this traffic before the specialist PNA wagons appeared. The converted wagons were fitted with extensions to the ends to further raise their height and were coded OBA, design code OB001E. Numbers were 110531/5/7/41/3/5/50/62/8/78/82/4/6/798, 110604/8/9/14/5/8/21/5/6/9/33/42/7/51/2/4/7/60/2/3/5/6/85, 110701/18/9/25/30/7/46/54/60/3/77/95. They were later bought by Plasmor and renumbered.

PLAS5276 (Taken at Biggleswade, 20/2/89)

Here we see one of the PNA vehicles being unloaded by mechanical grab. To facilitate this the hinged sides are tilted outwards; only when in transit and loaded are these sides fixed in the vertical position. Livery is as opposite. (Ref: W15104/DL)

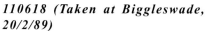

110618 (Taken at Biggleswade, 20/2/89)

Most of the dedicated OBAs to Plasmor traffic were painted in the company livery of orange/green/white. Note that the end extensions bring the wagon ends to the same height as the custom-built stock, seen to the right. (Ref: W15103/DL)

110754 (Taken at Biggleswade, 20/2/89)

Early conversions of the dedicated OBAs could be seen without the Plasmor livery. This one is in faded maroon livery with an unusual Railfreight legend on the side. The drop sides in four sections on these vehicles were not ideal for the loading and unloading of this traffic, the specialist design being favoured. (Ref: W15108/DL)

Section 38. Private Owner Bogie Steel Wagons

PDUF3023 (Taken at Hamworthy, 13/3/89)
These vehicles were similar in concept to the curtain sided vans in Section 34 but had platforms at each end to allow staff easy access to the hood mechanism. Livery is blue with black solebar and bogies. The POWELL DUFFRYN WAGON legend and logo are blue on white. (Ref: 15819/DL)

In addition to the vehicles mentioned in Section 34, pg. 76, there were other private owner wagons in service for transporting strip coil, most with covered load space for protection from the elements.

PDUF3043 (above) was built in 1986-88 by Powell Duffryn Ltd., Cardiff and was coded JSA. PDUF3008 to PDUF3017 were to design code JS044A and PDUF3018 to PDUF3042 and PDUF3044 to PDUF3062 were design code JS044B. They were seen on services from Port Talbot to the West Midlands and also recorded at Boston Docks.

PDUF3043 (opposite upper) was a one-off and also operated with the above fleet but had no hood. It was classified as a coil or slab steel convertible wagon and was coded JSA, design code JS048A.

33 80 474 6 410-6 (opposite centre) and 33 80 466 7 012-5 (opposite lower) were classed as steel hood wagons. Built in 1985 in Germany, with the then unusual three part

sliding hood, they subsequently became quite a familiar sight on the U.K. system.

In 1988 the number series was 33 80 474 6 000-5 to 33 80 474 6 049-2, though by 1992, this had been changed to 33 80 466 7 000-0 to 33 80 466 7 049-7. Initially they were in the ownership of V.T.G., as opposite centre, and were actually listed as operating on mainland Europe in 1990. By 1992, it appears that they had returned to the U.K. and were now operating as part of the Tiphook fleet.

Top. **PDUF3043 (Taken at Cardiff, 6/6/92)**
The one-off strip coil/slab JSA retained the end platforms but had no hood, thus allowing the internal load supports to be seen. Sides were blue, bogies black and lettering white.
(Ref: W17054/DL)

Centre. **33 80 474 6 410-6 (Taken at Warrington Dallam, 23/10/88)**
The number carried by this wagon in 1988 does not actually match the written record, so there may have been more than one renumbering phase, it was also coded PIA at that time. Livery for the hoods is silver with blue arrow, black solebar and bogies and white lettering.
(Ref: W14128/DL)

Below. **33 80 466 7 012-5 (Taken at Cardiff, 6/6/92)**
By the time of this view nearly four years later, the class had been coded IHA (design code IHE587). Livery is essentially as above but VTG has been replaced by TIPHOOK. (Ref: W17081/DL)

Section 39. P. W. Ballast Wagons (1)

DB973410 (Taken at Hoo Junction, 14/4/91)
The ZCV CLAM has totally fixed sides and ends and is heavily braced, as can be seen here. The brake cylinders, which were at one end of the HTV above solebar level (see Vol. 2, pg. 21.) are now below the floor. Livery is standard yellow/Rail Grey with black solebar and white lettering. The CLAM logo and code is Rail Grey. (Ref: W16583/DL)

The Civil Engineers' Department received very few totally new types into stock during the review period, instead relying mainly on rebuilds. One big rebuilding programme involved the old 21.5T HTO and HTV class.

DB973410 (above) is a ZCV CLAM for ballast and spoil duties. These came into service from 1989 onwards, the number range was DB973000 to DB973499, with delivery of many more projected vehicles being cancelled.

DB972522 (opposite upper) is the dropside version, designated ZBA RUDD. As this was not produced in a vacuum-braked version, it can be considered as the replacement design for the GRAMPUS. The vehicles appeared from 1989 onwards and were again part of a much curtailed rebuilding programme. The numbers were DB972000 to DB972799.

DB970049 (opposite centre) was very much a cheaper conversion option with cut down sides and the vacuum cylinders still in the original position. No air braked examples were built and the type was designated ZCV TOPE. Numbers for the curtailed batch were DB970000 to DB970059 and DB970100 to DB970849.

A small batch of ZCV TOPE wagons was allocated to the Electrification Department, probably for use on the ECML electrification scheme which occurred during the review period. LDB970854 (opposite lower) is an example, and as well as the different livery it is also devoid of the spoil flap modification at the ends of the wagon. Numbers were LDB970850 to LDB970854.

DB972522 *(Taken at Woking, 31/3/92)*
The ZBA RUDD has similar ends to the ZCV CLAM (opposite) but the sides are divided into three parts that can be lowered if necessary. Livery is as opposite. (Ref: W16695/DL)

DB970049 *(Taken at Welwyn Garden City, 30/5/92)*
The ZCV TOPE is really best used as a spoil wagon on large renewal jobs, although the load must be removed by grab as there are no longer any bottom doors. Compare the height with the ZKV BARBEL on the right. Livery is as opposite but with the addition of a small white oval. (Ref: W16937/DL)

LDB970854 *(Taken at Peterborough, 30/5/92)*
Exactly why the Electrification Engineers needed these wagons is unclear, but they were probably also used as spoil wagons. As with that above, they too represented the cheaper conversion option. Livery is Olive Green with black solebar and white lettering. (Ref: W16960/DL)

Section 40. P.W. Ballast Wagons (2)

DB988600 (Taken at Hither Green P.W. Depot, 5/5/89)
Having been little used as a ballast wagon, this sole prototype ZBA CARP appears to have been handed over to the C.E. plant section. One panel on each side of the wagon has been removed and there were channels welded to the floor as guides for a wheeled item of plant. Livery is yellow with black solebar and lettering. (Ref: W16421/DL)

The decision to go ahead with the CLAM/RUDD/TOPE programme of the previous section was almost certainly influenced by large numbers of recently rebuilt HTO and HTV wagons becoming available. However, before that programme commenced, certain prototypes were built.

DB988600 (above) was the solitary ZBA CARP built in 1983 by BREL, Shildon Works to Lot 4032. As can be seen here, it found another use in later years.

A number of ZBO GRAMPUS wagons were converted to ZBA HAKE (opposite upper) but this design seemed rather flimsy for the duties it was to perform and they appear to have suffered an early withdrawal. Numbers were DB986147, DB986208, DB986250 and DB986251.

A greater quantity of ZBO GRAMPUS were converted to ZBA RUDD, but not all seem to have been given new bodywork. DB986446 (opposite centre) is clearly marked RUDD but retains the original GRAMPUS bodywork whilst DB984849 (opposite lower) has the newer body. Numbers for this fleet as a whole were DB984075, DB984194,

DB984629, DB984788, DB984837/49/96, DB985544/61, DB985683, DB985728/73, DB985828, DB986446/50/65, DB986552, DB986689, DB986933/46, DB990109, DB990371/93, DB990630/87 and DB990770. They operate with the remainder of the RUDD fleet and are not on special duties.

Opposite Centre. *DB986446 (Taken at Aberdeen, 15/6/92)*
It is unclear exactly how many of the GRAMPUS rebuilt to RUDD retained the original bodywork, as here, particularly as there appears to be no separate design code. Livery is standard Yellow/ Rail Grey with RUDD in Grey. (Ref: W17130/DL)

Opposite Lower. *DB984849 (Taken at Reading, 16/5/92)*
For the untrained eye it is virtually impossible to tell the totally rebuilt GRAMPUS/RUDD apart from those rebuilt from hopper wagons other than by the number. Inspection of the brakegear however will reveal that Grampus rebuilds have eight shoe clasp brakes whilst the HTV rebuilds have four shoe push brakes. Livery is as above. (Ref: W16883/DL)

DB986147 *(Taken at Perth, 15/6/92)*
Before taking in new types, the B.R. authorities decided to try rebuilding the large GRAMPUS fleet. The ZBA HAKE rebuild seen here does not seem to have been a success. Livery is Olive Green with unusual yellow axleguards and white lettering. (Ref: W17146/DL)

Section 41. P. W. Ballast Wagons (3)

DC112039 (Taken at Hoo Junction Yard, 7/89)
These vehicles were not used in ballast trains on renewal projects. They were for conveying crushed granite from the quarry or, in this case, a shipment point, to an established tip where ballast hoppers etc., would be loaded. Livery is standard yellow/Rail Grey and SEAHORSE is in grey. (Ref: W16347/DL)

Air-braked former revenue wagons of the OBA, OCA and SPA types were transferred in sizeable quantities into C.E. stock during this review period. Later some were converted and rebuilt in order to perform new duties.

DC112039 (above) was an OCA originally (see section 5) and is seen here as a ZCA SEAHORSE, having been totally converted with new bodywork. Numbers for these were DC112029/39/40/2/50/9/64/8/70/3/6/8/82/4/94/5/8, DC112100/2/8/10/3/32/40/2/3/7/9/51/4/7.

Rather similar, but based on the OBA chassis, was the SEA URCHIN (opposite upper). These were still being converted in 1992 but known numbers at this time were DC110389, DC110619 and DC110630.

The ZAA PIKE fleet (opposite lower) consisted of transferred SPA types most of which were not converted in any great way during the review period. This comprised DC460003/5 – 8/11 – 7/9/20/2 – 35/7 – 9/41 – 6/8 – 52/5 – 60/3/5 – 7/9/71 – 81/3 – 5/7 – 92/4 – 8, DC460100/1/3 – 7/9 – 11/4 – 7/21/4 – 6/8 – 31/3/5/6/8 – 43/5 – 7/9/51/4 – 7/9/60/2 – 74/6 – 8/80/2/ - 5/7/9/91 – 9, DC460200 – 6/8/9/14/5/7/9/20/2/3/5/6/7/31 – 9/41 – 3/5 – 50/2 – 65/7/71 – 4/6 – 9/81/2/4 – 93/5 – 7, DC460300 – 6/8/9/11 – 4/7/8/21 – 9/31 in 1990.

Some of the PIKE type had their dropside doors permanently fixed and were recoded as SEAHARE (opposite centre). These were numbered DC460002/9/10/8/21/36/40/53/4/61/2/4/8/70/82/6/99, DC460102/8/12/22/34/44/8/50/2/3/8/61/75/9/81/6/8/90, DC460207/10/2/3/6/8/24/7/9/30/40/4/51/68 – 70/5/80/3/94/8/9, DC460307/10/5/6/9/20.

Opposite Top. *DC110619 (Taken at Peterborough, 30/5/92)*
Seen soon after delivery from rebuilding, these vehicles were very similar to the SEAHORSE class on the previous page but lacked the higher ends. Livery is standard yellow/Rail Grey but the number is on a black panel. (Ref: W16954/DL)

Opposite centre. *DC460299 (Taken at Leam-ington Spa, 1/4/92)*
The fixing of the doors is clearly seen on this vehicle and so is the recoding to ZCA, which presumably meant that it was for ballast carrying duties. Livery again is standard yellow/Rail Grey. (Ref: W16703/DL)

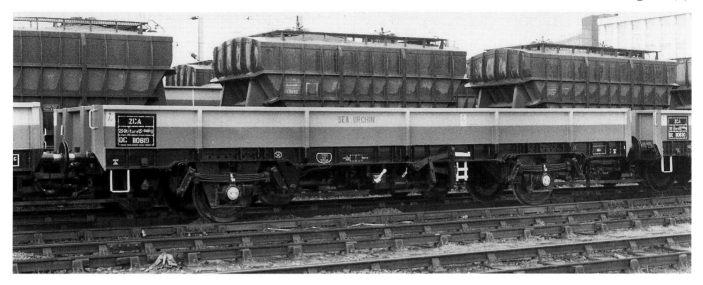

Right. ***DC460113 (Taken at Hitchin, 30/5/92)***
This appears to be a standard ZAA PIKE, but the lettering on the central panel is rather peculiar; "On hire from D - of - CE" - exactly who was hiring this vehicle? Standard yellow/ Rail Grey livery has been applied but PIKE is black and the extra panel is orange with black lettering.
(Ref: W16947/DL)

Section 42. P. W. Ballast Wagons (4)

DB987128 (Taken at Aberdeen, Craiginches, 15/6/92)
A number of Scottish based ballast wagons had a blue/white symbol on them and this can be observed to the left of this ZCV PLAICE example. Livery is a now rather tatty yellow/Rail Grey, the yellow being confined to the framing around the top of the wagon which acted as a step rail when the sides were in the lowered position. (Ref: W17135/DL)

For our final look at the Civil Engineers fleet, some older designs are featured.

The ZCV PLAICE wagons (above) were converted from SPV plate wagons back in the late 1970s and they could still be seen in service well into the review period. Numbers were DB987101 to DB987305.

Although ostensibly outmoded when compared with the more modern air-braked bogie hoppers (Vol. 3 pg. 94), both the ZEV CATFISH and ZFV DOGFISH (the latter illustrated opposite upper) could still be seen and some were even being given air through pipes for further use. 490 of the former and 840 of the latter were still extant at 1/4/94.

The bogie ballast hopper fleet from the late 1960s/early 1970s was still largely intact, including the SEACOW and the refurbished YHA WHALE class. Some of the smaller hoppers underwent conversion to YGB STINGRAY to provide lighting for ballast trains operating in remote areas. As the conversion was still going on in 1992, numbers, apart

from the one photographed, were not then available.

Finally the ubiquitous ZUV SHARK could still be found in some quantities and in various brake formats. The last batch of this type dates from 1962 and even earlier examples, such as DB993731 (opposite lower) built in 1956, could be seen. 155 out of a total of 216 of all types were still extant on 1/4/94.

Throughout the review period the civil engineers department had kept to fairly traditional practices and thus continued to require large numbers of wagons. Times were, however, changing and the increasing use of powered track machines, such as TRAMMs to carry bags of ballast, sleepers and trackwork, meant that wagon types would be reduced over the following decade.

DB993332 (Taken at Reading, 16/5/92)
The ZFV DOGFISH had served B.R. well since the late 1950s and continued to do so well into the 1990s. This photo shows an example of the type that was freshly repainted into the standard yellow/Rail Grey livery. The DOGFISH lettering is in grey. (Ref: W16911/DL)

DB982889 (Taken at Arbroath, 15/6/92)
To provide lighting for ballast hopper trains working in remote areas without access to a shore based power supply, some of the SEACOW hoppers were provided with generators. These were fitted into a casing on the end platform as seen here, and the wagons were appropriately reclassified as STINGRAY. Livery is standard yellow/Rail Grey but there is a red band to help identify them as special vehicles. (Ref: W17140/DL)

DB993731 (Taken at Middlesbrough, 13/6/92)
Although rarely seen on S.R. lines, the ZUV SHARK still had an important role to play in the C.E. fleet of the 1990s. This example, nearly 40 years old when photographed, is now seen in the standard departmental yellow/Rail Grey livery. Lettering is white. (Ref: W17095/DL)

Afterword

When this series of four volumes is considered as a whole, it is interesting to note that each one illustrates a distinct period in the history and development of the British railway freight wagon fleet.

Volume 1 covers a time where there was little apparent change. British Railway standard designs and pre-Nationalisation stock were still to be seen in large quantities and the fleet as a whole was very traditional. Changes there were, of course, though they mainly occurred in the background as new prototypes were quietly tested. The advent of air braking as a new common standard and innovative construction methods around this time signalled that the dawn of a new era was just over the horizon.

It was the period covered by Volume 2 that witnessed the emergence of the new fleets, those with air-brakes only, all of which operated as a separate but parallel entity to the surviving traditional vacuum fitted and unfitted fleets. That the old order could be seen running alongside the new

designs makes for unrivalled variety in wagon types in this review period.

Volume 3 saw the remains of the traditional fleet steadily ebb away whilst the air-braked fleet, rather than growing, went through a period of consolidation. The early 1980s actually witnessed a fresh optimism over the future of railfreight and further radical wagon designs emerged, although the dynamics of market forces put a dampener on sustained growth. In consequence, many of the new designs had a remarkably short life in their intended roles and by the time of this final volume, the diminishing of the air-braked fleet was all too apparent. Also covered in this volume is the virtual elimination of the traditional fleet, though in some instances there were some interesting survivors.

Throughout all four volumes one particular aspect is apparent: In general terms, the privately owned fleets have seen the most innovation in design and efficiency of usage. The newly nationalised British Railways back in 1948 tried,

ELC17512 (Taken at Hoo Junction Yard, 30/1/89)
Although very dirty to the point where no paintwork can be seen, this photographs links all four volumes in this series together and even up to the present day. Volume 1 began in 1968, the year this type was built. It was featured in Volume 2, page 56, and is now shown here for comparison. At the time of writing (2002), the class still performs the same duties it was introduced for and can be seen passing through Clapham Junction on a daily basis at around lunchtime. (Ref: W14864/DL).

REDA92545 (Taken at Hither Green, 12/4/92).
The self-discharging aggregate train was an extremely innovative concept which aimed to do away with the need to build expensive unloading plant and allow short term traffic opportunities to be developed at different locations. The wagon seen here is the 'business' end of the train where the conveyor belt arm is swung either left or right as required. The hoppers in the train are linked via a conveyor running beneath the solebars and certain wagons have motors to drive it.

as a matter of policy, to eliminate the private owner wagon totally, but failed in the longer term. British Rail's stated intention in the 1970s was to provide only general purpose railway owned stock in an attempt to woo customers, but it too largely failed.

From that point onward, Government, with the active co-operation of B. R., promoted the status of the private owner wagon and the railway owned fleets continued to decrease steadily right into the 1990s. That philosophy, coupled with technological advances, sowed the seeds and by the end of the 1980s totally new concepts such as the REDLAND self-discharge aggregate train (above) had been developed.

However, as in so many other ways, Privatisation of Britain's railways was to bring about some of the greatest changes to the system since pre-grouping days. It was about then that I put down my camera and ended almost a quarter of a century of personal wagon photography. That said, my interest in the wagon fleet has never waned and, although the variety is no longer there, perhaps in my retirement I can look forward to reading a new series written by those observers of more recent times.

Further Research.

In this work of four volumes, less than 800 photographs from my collection of some 17000 negatives have been published. This is of necessity due to commercial reasons, but I am pleased to still offer interested individuals the possibility of delving further into my library. Since volume one, imaging technology has changed quite remarkably and I am now able to make laser prints directly from negatives at much less cost than conventional photographic prints. Although the quality is not quite up to photographic standards, the images are certainly suitable for modelling or research purposes. Even those images which were taken under adverse lighting conditions and less suitable for publication in books, are now able to be printed with a little computer enhancement. So, although I can never promise an express response (we are, after all, talking about wagons here!), individuals should please feel free to contact me at the address shown below. For further information on this topic please refer to page 96 in either Volume 1 or Volume 2.

The author is currently undertaking research into railway wagons of the 1950s and 1960s with a view to publishing further titles;
Vol. 1. Wagons of the Beeching Years (1963 to 1968)
Vol. 2. Wagons of the Modernisation Years (1956 to 1962)
Vol. 3. Wagons of the Early BR Years (1948 to 1955)
Interested individuals who may be able to contribute material would be most welcome and should contact the author;
David Larkin
17 Albion Court
Albion Road
Sutton
Surrey SM2 5TB

Previous titles in this series

WORKING WAGONS Vol.1. 1968 - 1973
ISBN 0 9507960 6 9   **£11.95**

WORKING WAGONS Vol.2. 1974 - 1979
ISBN 0 9507960 7 7   **£11.95**

WORKING WAGONS Vol.3. 1980 - 1984
ISBN 0 9538448 2 X   **£12.95**

Each volume has 172 black and white photographs illustrating the BR wagon fleet in its everyday working role. With material drawn from the author's impressive photographic archive these books are an indispensible source of reference for modellers and historians specialising in this period.

Also from Santona Publications

You've seen the wagons, now build the layout!

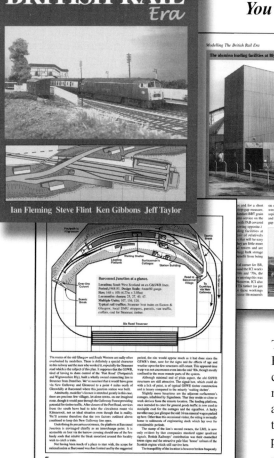

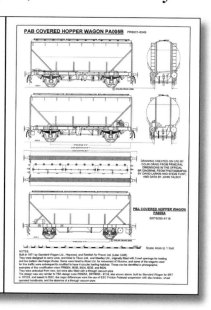

This fascinating book presents a comprehensive review of British Rail operations between 1964 and 1994 and examines how they can be adapted to create captivating, inspirational and authentic model railways. Selected prototype plans of BR freight wagons are featured along with modelling tips and numerous layout themes ideally suited to home locations. 96 pages with over 150 photographs and full colour sections.

MODELLING THE BRITISH RAIL ERA
ISBN 0 9507960 8 5   **£14.95**